THE
TABLOID
BIBLE

THE
TABLOID
BIBLE

Nick Page

HarperCollins*Publishers*

HarperCollins*Publishers*
77–85 Fulham Palace Road, London W6 8JB

First published in Great Britain in 1998 by
HarperCollins*Publishers*

3 5 7 9 10 8 6 4 2

A catalogue record for this book is
available from the British Library

ISBN 000 274022 2

Printed and bound in Great Britain by
Woolnough Bookbinding Ltd, Irthlingborough, Northamptonshire

THE SCROLL

HELLO WORLD

God Creates The World
And it only takes six days!

In an unparalleled moment of creativity, God has created the world.

"It's a remarkable achievement," said Adam (2 days). "Especially when you consider that he took Sunday off."

So far plans for the new world are sketchy although God (infinity) is rumoured to be planning a "state of perpetual bliss".

Critics, however, point to some dangers. "I'm not entirely convinced it's a good idea for the lamb to lie down with the lion," said a nearby serpent. "The lion has been giving the lamb some very funny looks."

Details

There have also been some questions about specific details.

"I can't quite see the point of wasps," said Adam. "And I must admit that the duck-billed platypus looks as if it has been simply thrown together. Other than that, though, the whole thing is a paradise."

The main development in the world is the Garden of Eden, where Adam is to live and look after the animals.

Adam, when asked about his plans, said, "Well, there's plenty of room for me to work in. In particular I'd like to put in a patio and possibly a bit of a rockery."

- Adam to name the animals
- Big hot shiny thing is called the "sun"
- Wet stuff is water – don't put your head under – official
- Morning will always start at dawn, despite pleas to make it later

Adam Names The Animals

Adam has been given the responsibility of naming the beasts in the new world.

"It's a big job," said Adam (3 days). "Especially the insects. The trouble is they won't keep still."

Names under consideration include "Elephant", "Camel", "Simpson's Gazelle" and "Norman".

"So far all I've managed is 'cat', 'dog' and 'you irritating little swine'. Although I think 'flea' may be the preferred choice for the last one."

Thank God for Sunday

SCROLL EXCLUSIVE

God invents the weekend

After his exertions in completing creation in just six days, God rested on the seventh day.

Now he is urging all creation to follow his example.

"The seventh day should be a day of rest," he said. "No one wants to work all the time. Apart from Richard Branson, and I haven't invented him yet. Ideally, it should be a time for recharging the batteries, for thinking about the important things in life."

"I'm going to use the day for quiet reflection," agreed Adam (1 week)."And for going to a car boot sale if anyone's having one."

Meat-free Diet

God has declared that the Garden of Eden is to be a vegetarian zone. Guidelines have been published allowing man to eat "any seed-bearing plants or fruit" and animals to eat any foliage.

Adam stated, "This is fine by me. After all, we're supposed to be living together in perfect harmony. I think if we started eating one another that would put a bit of a strain on relationships."

The lion and the lamb were unavailable for comment.

What do you think?

Paradise on earth? Or just "quite nice"?

Send your comments, moos, barks, grunts or strange buzzy noises to:

The Scroll

Just to the Left of the Tree of Life, Garden of Eden, The Near East.

The Scroll

The Scroll is printed on environmentally friendly fig-leaves.

Trees Of Good And Evil

A tree in the centre of the garden has been designated as a nature reserve.

"You can eat of any of the fruit of the garden, but not of the tree of knowledge of good and evil," said God. When pressed further on why this should be so, he said, "You just need to trust me on this one."

Adam said, "It's OK by me. Anyway, we can eat the fruit from the tree of life, so that's OK. It's especially good in a crumble."

Serpent Questions Fruit Policy

In a shock statement tonight, the Serpent has gone on record as questioning God's policy with regard to the trees in the garden.

"Far be it from me to question the divine authority," he said. "But I think we need to get some more answers about this fruit. Is it really as dangerous as we are told?"

"I, for one, would like to see more tests being done."

When it was pointed out that the only real test would be for someone to eat it, the Serpent smiled and slid away.

HE AND SHE
God Creates Adam Upgrade

God has created a companion for Adam. Called Eve, the new creation is noticeably curvier and more aerodynamic.

Among the improvements are more storage space and significantly less hair on the upper body.

"I think she's wonderful," said a completely love-struck Adam (3 weeks). "I was getting a bit lonely there, what with only the duck-billed platypus to talk to."

Ribs

According to informed sources, Eve was created from one of Adam's ribs.

"I'm not sure why God needed a bit of me to start from," said Adam. "Maybe you have to start with some base material, like yoghurt. I don't know what happened to the other rib but I've noticed the lion looking a bit shifty recently."

Adam was put under general anaesthetic while the event took place.

"Not only was the operation completely painless," he said, "but there wasn't even a waiting list."

Version 2.0

"I'm delighted to be here," said Eve (30 mins). "I don't think of myself as subservient. I think I'm more of an upgrade. Man 2.0, if you like."

Eve also believes that she will be able to help out around the garden.

"I want to help Adam as best I can," she told us.

"I'm looking forward to life here in the garden. The fruit looks lovely, especially the apples."

WOULD YOU ADAM AND EVE IT!

First Humans Expelled From Garden

Adam and Eve have been expelled from the Garden of Eden for eating forbidden fruit.

Although God had prohibited them from eating the fruit of the knowledge of good and evil, they did just that.

"It was Eve's fault," said Adam. "She told me to do it."

"It was the snake's fault," said Eve. "He tempted me." The snake refused to comment.

Challenge

Their actions can be seen as a direct challenge to God's authority and will come as a terrible blow to the future of the whole mankind project.

"At the moment we're launching an appeal," said Adam (1 month), "but if that is unsuccessful, we will just have to accept whatever the consequences might be. It's a tragedy because there is still so much to do. For a start I haven't finished the naming yet. I've only got as far as 'bear'."

Temptation

Some have questioned whether God was asking for trouble.

"Every creature in my earth has free will," said God. "Adam and Eve were offered a simple choice. It wasn't about prohibition, it was about who they wanted to be in charge. They have made their choice. Now they have to face the consequences.

"In the future, mankind will have more and more of these choices. They will become like gods. It's just a shame that they will never be very godly."

Clothing Invented

The first signs of this amazing fall from grace came about when Adam invented clothing. He immediately fashioned a simple loin cloth out of fig-leaves.

"I suddenly felt this sense of shame," he said. "I felt I wanted to cover things up. The only thing I could find was fig-leaves."

"I would have preferred something in black, or possibly turquoise," added Eve. "And ideally, I think it needs a matching handbag to really carry it off."

Skin

Before they left the garden, God helped them to replace their leaves with skin tunics.

"They're still my children," he said. "I wouldn't want them to get cold."

"It was good of God to replace the fig-leaves," confirmed Adam. "We were a bit worried about what would happen in the autumn."

Punishment Outlined

Now they must face their punishment. Although details are sketchy it is understood that their actions will have the following horrific consequences:

- Original sin.
- Immediate expulsion from the Garden of Eden.
- Painful child-bearing for all women.
- Hard work and painful toil for all men.
- Sickness (especially bunions).
- Mime artists.
- Death.

The last item is particularly confusing.

"We don't know anything about death," said Adam. "We don't know what it means."

A sad God replied, "You will."

Oi! Mind That Flaming Sword!

Angels Guard the Garden Gates

Following the dramatic fall of Adam and Eve, angels have been put on duty at the entrance to the Garden of Eden. The guardians have been variously described as "Angels", "Great Winged Creatures" and, "What The Heck Is That?"

The guardians are required to stop anyone re-entering and eating from the tree of life.

"Anyone who discovers the Garden of Eden will be turned back," confirmed God. "Man just isn't up to earthly paradise. They will have to make do with Butlins."

SCROLL SPOT
Shock Lunch

In a possibly related incident today, the lion ate the lamb.

CAIN IN THE NECK

Cain Kills Abel In Row Over Favouritism

In what appears to be a premeditated attack, Cain has killed his brother Abel.

The two fell out over their sacrifices to God. "Apparently the sacrifice of Cain (30) was rejected by God, whilst Abel's (25) was accepted," said one witness.

"I don't think it was anything to do with the sacrifice itself. I think it was more Cain's behaviour. He has a really serious attitude problem."

Lured

Angered by his rejection, Cain lured his brother out to the fields where he killed him. At first he denied having done the deed.

"Since he was trying to fool God, it was a bit futile," said the witness. "It's pointless trying to lie to a being who knows everything."

'Murder'

Officials are left trying to come to terms with the newness of the event.

"This is the first act of violence we've witnessed," said the investigating team. "In fact, it's the first act of violence anyone has ever witnessed. Originally we termed it 'very-bad-deed-which-ended-with-the-loss-of-some-one's-life', but we gradually whittled that down to 'murder'."

It is hoped that the new name will not be needed again.

"Let's just hope this is an isolated incident. I don't want to see it on my patch again."

JUDGEMENT ON CAIN

Cain Given Supernatural Electronic Tag

In punishment for killing his brother Abel, Cain has been banished from the presence of God.

In a judgement which echoes that handed out to his parents, Cain will have to leave the land where he is settled and wander the earth.

Marked

For his own protection, Cain has been given a mark from God.

"It's kind of like early electronic tagging," said a bystander. "It's a warning really. Anyone who kills Cain will suffer dire consequences."

Following his expulsion Cain has entered the land of Nod, East of Eden.

City

Rumours are that he has established the first city and named it after his son Enoch.

"Just as well his son wasn't called 'A Bit of a Dump'," commented one resident. "Or worse still, 'Kettering'."

The Scroll
Audited Circulation 3 (Was 4, but one of our subscribers has just been 'very-bad-deed-which-ended-with-the-loss-of-someone's-lifed').
Write to us as soon as writing is invented at:
The Scroll, 24 A Long Row of Houses, Chipping Enoch, Enochshire, Land of Nod.

ARKING MAD!
Father Of Three Builds Bumper Boat In His Backyard

Animals Missing

In a bizarre series of kidnappings, pairs of animals have gone missing from zoos and wildlife parks throughout the country.

"We're baffled," admitted one distraught zoo owner. "Virtually all of our breeding pairs have disappeared. We've only got a couple of Unicorns left."

Police are following the theory that it is the work of animal rights activists.

Weather
A sunny day everywhere, with possible sandstorms later. Min. 120°. Air Quality: poor.
Outlook: changeable.

A previously respectable citizen is building the world's biggest boat – in his garden! And all because he thinks a flood's coming.

What is more, he has no previous experience of boat building and lives hundreds of miles from the sea!

Noah (534) said, "You're all doomed. God will save myself and my family, but the rest of you will be drowned."

A neighbour commented, "I can't believe it's happening. He's always seemed such a quiet man. And I'm sure he doesn't have planning permission."

Judgement
So why is he doing this? Nutty Noah is convinced that the world is about to be caught up in a cataclysmic flood.

"God's judgement cannot be escaped," he told our reporter. "The world is a sinful place and it will be washed clean."

Design
When it is finished, the boat will be the biggest vessel ever made, beating the previous record holder – the Mesopotamian Queen Nefertiti II – by hundreds of metres.

However, naval experts were sceptical of its design. "This is not a boat, it's a box," said a source at the admiralty. "He won't be able to steer it and there isn't even a sail."

But Noah refused to give in. "What do I want to steer it for?" he replied. "There won't be anywhere to steer it to. All it has to do is ride out the flood."

A government spokesman commented, *"This is a desert. We don't get many floods round here."*

LAND AHOY!
Dove Disappears In Test For Dry Land

After nearly a year, the flood is over. The ark has landed and a dove sent out from the ark early yesterday morning has not returned – proof that the waters have subsided.

"We've waited a long time," said a relieved Captain Noah (535). "It's good to be back on dry land again."

The ark came to rest on Mount Ararat. Noah and his family (and all the animals) emerged to find themselves on top of the mountain.

"We're very happy to be home," said Shem, Noah's eldest son. "We were getting a bit low on supplies and were very tempted to start eating some of the livestock. Not only that, but quite early in the voyage someone mislaid the woodworm. Another few days and they could have eaten through the hull."

When asked for his future plans, Noah said, "We have to breed, multiply and fill the earth again, which is going to be a bit of an effort with my dodgy back. But first of all, I'm going to have a drink."

Rainbow

After Noah performed a sacrifice, God promised never again to purge humanity.

"The Lord has promised that he will not do this again," reported Noah. "Despite what men are like in the future, never again will the living things be destroyed in this way. He sent us a rainbow as a sign – every time we see a rainbow in the future we are to remember God's promise to all mankind."

Grape Expectations

Scientists are investigating a possible new use for grapes. They are experimenting with turning the popular fruit into a drink.

"The grapes give off a rather lovely tasting juice," explained a scientist. "But it tastes even better when you leave it for a while in vats."

So far several tasters have tried the new drink – or "wine" as it's being termed – but most of them are still unconscious. The only one to have recovered said, "It's got an intense, woody flavour with undertones of tar." He then went off complaining of a headache.

TOWERING CONFUSION!

Tower Of Babel Crashes Project Ends In Chaos

The Tower of Babel project has collapsed due to what the management team called "an unprecedented communication breakdown".

"I knew we were running into problems when suddenly we couldn't agree on the word for 'brick'," said one builder.

"I asked the bloke next to me to pass me his trowel and he hit me. Apparently in his language I said 'Your grandmother has the face of a warthog.' One minute we were all speaking a common language, the next we couldn't understand a word the other person was saying. It was a nightmare."

Scale

Observers believe that this sudden confusion came about because of the scale of the project. The Tower of Babel was intended to reach heaven and dominate the whole of creation.

"It was our 'god' project," said one builder. "This was going to unify mankind and bring us all together. Now it's like we're further apart than ever."

Conspiracy

Various theories have been put forward as to where all these different languages came from. The most common theory is that God sabotaged the project because of man's arrogance.

"It was industrial espionage!" exclaimed one investor. "As a manufacturer of bricks, this project was going to make me very, very rich. I'm thinking of suing. I just don't know how you register a claim against the supreme being."

The project was finally abandoned yesterday after a statement by the managing director at a packed shareholders meeting.

"Xxyshhibbothuth mi varg," he said.

No translation was available.

HERE TODAY, AND GONE GOMORRAH!

Cities Destroyed By Rain Of Fire

Sodom and Gomorrah have been destroyed by a hail of fire and brimstone. There is nothing left of the cities that once stood there except for smouldering ashes and molten rock.

"The cities have been destroyed by God as a punishment for their crimes," said Lot (60), whose family was the only one to escape the holocaust. "It was a miracle that we were able to get out."

Strangers

The dreadful story began yesterday evening when two strangers arrived at the city gates. Lot, whose family had settled outside the city, offered them hospitality.

"The next thing I knew," said Lot, "there were hundreds of the townspeople outside, demanding that we were to hand the strangers over to them. They said they 'wanted to show them a thing or two'. And I don't think they were talking about their stamp collection."

The mob insisted that Lot hand over the visitors so that they could have sex with them! Lot tried to calm the mob down but they were too drunk.

"The situation was getting out of hand," he said. "They were determined to have their way. It's always been the same in this city. Anyone visiting would either be molested, attacked or mugged. Sometimes all at once. Just going to the supermarket meant taking an armed guard and a big bucket of cold water."

Angels

Little did the townspeople realize that these strangers were not victims but avengers!

"I thought the people were going to get us all," said Lot, "when the men pulled us back inside.

Continued on page 18

Continued from page 17

"Then there was this incredibly bright light and the townspeople were wandering around blinded. All you could hear was people cursing and screaming and bumping into things. I realized these visitors were angels. They told me to escape at once."

Even then his sons-in-law didn't believe him.

"I was only able to escape with my wife and daughters before the fire came."

Power

Within minutes, fire and brimstone were raining down on the hapless inhabitants of the cities. As dawn rose, Sodom and Gomorrah were razed to the ground in an awesome display of God's power. In the end, their crimes have been repaid with interest.

"This place has been the toilet bowl of humanity for ages," said Lot. "I think God finally pulled the chain."

Lot's Wife Is A-Salt-ed.

Lot, the only man to survive the disaster at Sodom, lost his wife during the tragedy.

"We were running away when, unfortunately, my wife couldn't resist stopping and looking back. She was immediately turned into a pillar of salt."

She will not be forgotten.

"For one thing I took a bit of her arm to put on my chips," said Lot.

Now Lot and his daughters are living in caves in the hills.

His daughters said, "I don't know what's going to become of us. There is no one left to marry us and carry on the race. We're going to have to do a bit of lateral thinking."

Why Not Take My Daughters?

Did Lot offer his daughters to the mob?

Among the rumours coming out of the disaster zone was the story that Lot offered his daughters to the lust-crazed mob.

When the mob came to the house they wanted to have sex with the male visitors, but according to one unnamed source, Lot tried to offer them his daughters instead.

If this is true, then it is obvious that Lot was not saved because of his personal holiness. Anyone willing to sacrifice their own daughters to the mob is a buffoon, incapable of thinking straight.

Lot refused to comment.

"I've had a hard day," was all that he would say.

Worried About Your Relatives?

If you have relatives living in either Sodom or Gomorrah, you have two choices.
1. Call the government hotline 002 1136 77899
2. Accept that everybody has been pounded into oblivion, and collect the life insurance.

THIS HAS BEEN A GOVERNMENT ANNOUNCEMENT.

Not Even Ten Good Men!
Abram pleads with God for the City

Abram has revealed how he pleaded with God to save the city.

"God told me that he was going to destroy Sodom and Gomorrah," said Abram (99). "But he agreed that if there were just ten upright men in the city he would spare it. Unfortunately I was being optimistic."

Visit

Abram (99) had been visited by the angels earlier in the day.

"Three men came to visit me. I didn't realize then who they were. It was only after they'd accepted my hospitality, that I realized I was not entertaining ordinary travellers. The Lord told me what he was going to do to the cities and made me other promises as well."

"I would tell you the details, but you'd only laugh."

90 YEAR OLD GIVES BIRTH

Experts Question Availability Of Fertility Rituals

A woman has given birth to a baby boy at the age of 90. What's more, her husband is 10 years older than her!

The couple, who only last year hit the headlines when they were involved in the events leading up to the destruction of Sodom, are now the proud parents of a baby boy called Isaac.

"We were told last year that this was going to happen," said Abraham (100). "My wife just laughed at the time, but as usual, God has had the last laugh."

Questions

Not everyone, however, is celebrating the event.

"I think it raises some serious questions about fertility rituals," said one local priest. "We make a living out of persuading people that using our rituals will result in the patter of tiny feet. What does it do to our business if the God of Abraham just goes around promising children without them having to pay anything? It's like he's making up the rules as he goes along.

"There are also serious questions as to whether it's right that anyone should have a baby at 90. I mean by the time the lad's old enough to kick a football around, the father is going to be 107. He's not going to want to take junior to the park, is he? The only dribbling he's going to do is the senile kind."

Surprise

"It's as big a surprise to us as to anyone," responded Abraham. "But where God is involved human age doesn't come into it."

Abraham and Sarah are as delighted as any 20-year-olds.

"Who would have thought that I would ever have a child?" said Sarah (90). "God has given me something to laugh about, and everyone who hears about it will join in the joke!"

Ishmael Leaves Home

Abraham's eldest son, Ishmael, has left home.

Ishmael's mother was Hagar, a servant of Abraham's. The boy and his mother left Abraham's home amid rumours of a falling out with Sarah.

"She insisted that the boy leave," said one member of the household. "There was no way she was going to have her son share the inheritance with Ishmael. Abraham was very upset about it."

"God said that this boy, too, would be the father of a great nation," said Abraham. "I was upset to see him go, but once Sarah makes up her mind she's difficult to budge. You know what 90-year-old women are like. Especially 90-year-olds with post natal-depression."

Despair

Abraham gave them some food to take with them, but it ran out when they were in the desert. In despair, Hagar left her boy under a bush.

"I couldn't bear to see him die!" she explained. "But then God spoke to me and said that he was going to make Ishmael the father of a great nation. Then God showed me to a well, so we were saved."

Ishmael is reported to be doing well and to have taken up archery.

BACK FROM THE BRINK!

Son Saved From Sacrifice Scenario

In a bizarre last-minute escape, Abraham was stopped from killing his son in a sacrifice. The old man, who had waited one hundred years for his wife to give birth, believed that God told him to sacrifice the boy.

"I don't really know what it was all about," said Abraham (110). "I thought it was some kind of test. I couldn't believe that God wanted me to sacrifice the boy he himself had given us. It would have broken my heart."

Abraham took the boy and built the altar in the land of Moriah. Then he TIED his son to the altar and GRABBED a knife.

But just before he was going to strike, God stopped his hand.

Blessings

"God said that as I had proved my faithfulness, he would shower blessings on me. I looked round and saw a ram, caught by its horns in a bush. I sacrificed that instead."

"Who knows what was going on in the mind of God?" said Abraham. "All I know is that it's a terrible thing as a father to have to give up your child. Perhaps one day, in this place God will know how I felt."

Abraham has subsequently turned down offers for the film rights.

ISAAC GETS THE HUMP

Servant Finds Wife Watering Camels

"I found a wife for Isaac by divine guidance!" That's the claim of a servant of Abraham, sent to find a wife for his master's younger son.

"Abraham told me to go and find a wife from his native people. He said that an angel would guide me. I figured since he'd met a few angels in his time he'd know what he was talking about."

The servant claims he met the girl as she watered his camels.

"It was very easy to find her," he said. "I think the camels broke the ice. Which makes a nice change from them breaking wind."

Niece

When the servant asked who the girl was, he discovered that she was RELATED to Isaac. "It was incredible. I'd gone hundreds of miles to this strange land and the first person I meet is Abraham's niece."

The girl, whose name is Rebekah, returned with the servant and married Isaac immediately.

"It was love at first sight," said the servant. "Even the camels went all misty eyed."

Abraham Dies

Abraham has died at the age of 175.

Unusually, it was the last one hundred years of his life that were the most eventful. Originally a native of Ur of the Chaldees, he left there when he was a mere 75, with his nephew, Lot. Eventually they were to part, Lot towards Sodom and Abraham to Canaan.

"God promised that his descendants would be as numerous as the grains of sand," said one friend of the family. "He is the father of nations. Just as well he doesn't have to remember their birthdays."

BIRTHRIGHT ROBBERY!

Son Swaps It All For Soup

A famished son was TRICKED out of his inheritance – all because he was desperate for soup! And what's more, the person who tricked him was his TWIN BROTHER!

The soup-er trickster was Jacob (20), who conned his twin Esau (work it out) out of his birthright.

"I'd just got in from hunting," explained a red-faced Esau, "and I was absolutely starving. Isaac had cooked up this great soup, with lentils and everything. I felt like I was at death's door, so I agreed to exchange my birthright for as much soup as I could eat. It seemed like a good deal at the time. And I did negotiate for an extra bread roll."

Red Head

Now Esau, who with his twin Jacob is the son of Isaac, and grandson of Abraham, is claiming he was attracted by the colour.

"When I was born I was covered in red hair," explained the ginger nut. "It's always made me a bit hot-headed. When I saw this soup it was red-brown. Just the colour I like. I couldn't resist it."

Grasping

Although the two are twins, Esau is the eldest by a few seconds. Jacob followed Esau into the world by grabbing onto his brother's heel. "He's always been a grasping individual," claimed Esau. "But this is a new low."

Blessing In Disguise

In a second food-related fraud, Jacob has swindled his brother out of his father's blessing.

The blessing – a powerful prayer promising prosperity and a good life – should have been bestowed on Esau, but the near-blind Isaac blessed his younger son by mistake!

"Isaac asked Esau to make him a stew," explained one servant. "While Esau was off doing that, Jacob dressed up as Esau and took a dish his mother prepared for him to Isaac. The old man is as blind as a bat and was somehow fooled into thinking that Jacob was Esau. So he blessed him instead."

Furry Fraud

Now *The Scroll* can reveal how the fraud was perpetrated.
★ Jacob dressed in his brother's clothes.
★ He covered his neck and arms in goatskin.
★ Isaac felt these hairy arms and thought it was Esau. "Isaac was a bit suspicious, because Jacob couldn't do the voice," said the servant. "But when he felt the arms he thought it had to be Esau. Esau is a seriously hairy bloke."

Discovery

It wasn't until Esau returned from the hunting field that Isaac discovered his hairy mistake.

"When Esau came in, Isaac realized what he'd done. He trembled all over. But it was too late. A blessing, once given, cannot be taken back."

The blessing means that Jacob will now be master of his brother. Esau will have to live by the sword.

"Esau will always be a hunter now," said the servant. "And the first thing he's going to hunt is his brother."

TWO WIFE SENTENCES!

Arch-trickster Tricked By The Headdress

New Questions Over The Role Of The Veil

The man who tricked his brother out of his inheritance has been tricked himself into marrying the wrong woman.

Jacob (47) is well known to readers of *The Scroll* as the tricky twin, who duped his brother. Now he has been tricked into marrying the sister of the woman he wanted for his bride. And what is more, he's going to have to give up another seven years of service to get the woman he really wants!

The tables were turned by his own uncle Laban. In a pre-nuptual agreement, Jacob agreed to work for seven years to gain Rachel (16), Laban's daughter. But on the wedding night he realized that he'd been tricked. He'd actually married Laban's other daughter, Leah (18).

"I don't know what he's complaining about," said Laban. "Leah has lovely eyes. And anyway, it is not the custom around here to marry off the younger daughter before the eldest. You have to start at the top and work down."

Custom

It was local custom that caused the problem. According to tradition, all brides are kept fully veiled until their wedding night.

"I blame the veil," said our fashion correspondent. "Not only does it carry the potential for mix-ups of this kind, it's terribly passé. With a thick enough veil and baggy clothing, there could be anybody under there. Jacob simply couldn't see who he was marrying. It could have been a camel for all he knew."

New Agreement

Now Jacob has agreed to work a further seven years for Rachel – the bride he really wanted.

"We have agreed that Jacob can marry my other daughter at the end of this week," confirmed Laban. "After that he owes me another seven years' work. And I promise that this time he will get the bride he wants. No, really."

WOULD EWE BELIEVE IT?

Genetic Engineering Produces Abnormal Numbers Of Black Sheep

IN WHAT is believed to be the first example of genetic engineering, ewes and she-goats have given birth to speckled and spotted offspring.

The process stands to make Jacob (54) extremely rich.

Deal

The process was discovered by Jacob after a deal between him and his uncle Laban.

"Jacob is planning to leave Laban and return to his homeland," said a shepherd. "They agreed that Jacob could take with him any black sheep or spotted goat from the flocks."

Once the agreement was in place, Jacob went to work. He made sure that the goats mated whilst looking at striped pieces of wood. This affected them so much they produced abnormally high numbers of striped or spotted kids. He also ensured that the sheep mated while looking at black goats. They gave birth to high numbers of black sheep. Jacob claims the process was given to him by God in a dream.

"It only goes to show that we are deeply affected by our viewing," said the shepherd.

Excitement

The discovery has led to a lot of excitement among scientists.

"I'm currently training a duck to stare at an orange," said one expert. "The idea is to breed ducks with the *duck à l'orange* taste built in."

Another scientist is playing his beef herd Leonard Cohen records.

"*By the time they get to the abbatoir, they can't wait to be slaughtered,*" he explained.

Rarity

It is another turn in the increasingly twisted saga of Jacob and his relations. "Laban must have thought he was on to a good thing – because these kind of animals are a rarity," said one expert. "But once again, Jacob has proved that you can't keep a good trickster down. He's built up huge flocks through this process."

Laban was unavailable for comment last night. "I expect he's feeling a bit sheepish," said his spokesman.

SCROLL SPORTS
All the Action All the Time

Jacob Transfer

Jacob (60) has left his uncle's team after the breakdown of negotiations over a new contract.

After twenty years away he is reported to be seeking reconciliation with his father Isaac, and brother Esau.

"I think he's had enough of tricking and being tricked," said one observer.

Relations had been increasingly strained between the two of them, centred mainly around Jacob's wage demands and Laban's managerial style.

The tension culminated in Jacob's sudden departure.

Treaty

"There was a bit of a row over some suspected missing property," reported a servant. "But the two have made a pact now. They have agreed not to attack each other. I know that they are related, but lots of people have problems getting on with their in-laws. *Although I do admit signing a peace treaty is a little unusual.*"

Jacob Injured In All-night Wrestling Bout
Who Was The Mystery Wrestler?

A wrestler who fought all night with Jacob has been offered a six-figure sum to turn professional.

"The guy has star quality," said promoter King Don of Jabbok. "Mystery, technique, he's got it all. I can offer him a huge purse. No money, just a flipping big purse."

The wrestling match took place the night before Jacob was due to meet his brother Esau again. As Jacob recounts his story, he spent the night in physical struggle, wrestling with a being he referred to as "a man". In the end, the figure dislocated Jacob's hip.

Experience

"It was a weird experience," said Jacob. "I fought as hard as I could. Before he disappeared, he blessed me, and told me that I would no longer be called Jacob. He didn't say what I should be called."

Jacob is in no doubt as to the identity of "the man" with whom he wrestled that night. *"I have seen God face to face," he said, "and I survived."*

Stress

Others, however, claim it never really happened.

"In certain times of heightened stress," said one psychiatrist, "it can feel almost physical. I remember during one stressful period, I dreamt I was being forced to swallow an enormous naan bread. When I woke I found I'd eaten the duvet. I can't believe that God would wrestle anyone."

When asked to explain Jacob's dislocated hip, the psychiatrist said, "He probably fell over getting out of the bath or something."

Jacob refused to be cowed. *"All of us wrestle with God sometimes,"* he said. *"But not many of us face to face."*

Re-united!
Brothers Make Up After Years Apart

Twenty years after leaving Canaan, Jacob was reunited with his brother Esau. Old feuds were forgotten, as Esau rushed forward to meet his brother and threw his arms around Jacob's neck.

"For a moment we thought he was going to strangle him, but it turned out to be a hug," said one relieved onlooker.

WAS THIS THE UNKINDEST CUT OF ALL?

Shechemites Slain While Recuperating

Simeon and Levi Avenge Rape Ordeal

The entire male inhabitants of a town have been slain while they were recuperating from CIRCUMCISION.

The invalids did not realize the mass operations were just part of a cunning plan.

"It was the tip of the iceberg, as it were," said a source.

Revenge

"This was a revenge attack, pure and simple. Prince Shechem (30) had forced his attentions on Dinah (16), the daughter of Jacob. I think in a strange way he really cared about her, but that doesn't excuse his conduct. He even took her back into the town with him."

After his crime was discovered, Shechem promised Jacob he would do anything in order to marry her.

Circumcision

Jacob's sons insisted that Shechem, and all the men in his town, should be circumcised, according to their custom.

"Naturally, most of them weren't very happy about it," said a witness. "I mean, it's one thing to pay your council tax, it's another thing entirely to have small, but significant parts of your todger hacked off.

"But they thought that if they did that then all the wealth of Jacob would come to them. It's not exactly a normal way of encouraging inward investment, but there you are."

In fact the operations were nothing more than a

Continued on page 27

Continued from page 26

cunning and vicious plan concocted by Simeon and Levi, Jacob's sons. While all the men were recovering in bed, they rampaged through the town, entering every house and killing each and every man.

"The townsfolk should have seen it coming. They were complete idiots. Well, not quite complete..."

Immobilized

"You shouldn't underestimate how painful an operation this is," explained a doctor, ignoring the fact that our reporter spent most of the time with his legs crossed and his eyes watering.

"For a few days a man can hardly walk, let alone defend himself against two fully armed attackers. These men were completely immobilized. They were sitting targets. Or lying down, whimpering, targets, rather."

Jacob "Furious"

"Jacob (80) is reported to be absolutely furious," said one family source. "It places the whole family at risk of reprisal from those around them. The trouble is, his sons believed that their sister had been treated like a whore. There was no way they were ever going to let Shechem marry her after what he did."

Jacob

Some sources are even placing the blame on Jacob.

"He was told by God to settle in Bethel. It was his choice to stop here. He must now face the consequences of his own decision."

Dinah was not consulted and was not available for comment.

THE SCROLL SAYS

When Will It End?

The latest outrage makes depressingly familiar reading.

It seems that, ever since the expulsion from the Garden, the story of mankind has been nothing but a sordid tale of rape, incest, sexual deviancy, murder and revenge.Something must be done.

We need laws. We need justice. We need guidance.

One day, maybe, someone will come to show us the right way to live.

Perhaps, one day, we might even listen.

We at *The Scroll* are committed to recording history as it happened. We are dealing with human beings. And human beings do terrible things sometimes.

For now, we will continue to do our duty and report the facts without sensationalism. (See, for example our story 'Rape, Pillage and Murder', complete with 37 illustrations and a pop-up diagram.)

No, don't thank us. We're just doing our job.

The Scroll. The paper that's not afraid to use the word "circumcision".

SCROLL SPOT

Jacob has changed his name, after receiving instructions from God.

"I was thinking of being called The Artist Formally Known As Jacob," he said.

"But God told me that from now on my name is to be Israel.

"Apparently he's going to name a nation after me."

COULD THEY BE LION?
Mystery Death Of Jacob's Son

Joseph – the seventeen-year-old son of Jacob – has been killed by a lion. But police are keeping the case open.

"We are treating the death as suspicious," said Chief Inspector Zibeon of the Canaan Police. "Although the lad's tunic has been discovered, there are a lot of questions still to be asked.

"For one thing the body has not been recovered, and forensics are suspicious of the bloodstains on the coat. For the moment our investigations will continue."

Coat
Joseph's death comes amid rumours of bad feeling between him and his brothers. "Jacob has twelve sons," said a friend of the family. "But Joseph was always his favourite. He even had a multi-coloured coat made up for him. The lad was immensely proud of this coat, although I always thought it made him look like a bit of a hippy."

Dream
It wasn't just the coat that caused rifts between the brothers.

"The lad was always a bit of a dreamer," said our contact. "And some of his dreams made him out to be overly important. He had one dream that seemed to foretell that all his family would end up bowing down to him. Needless to say this was not well received by his brothers. "

Death Riddle
On the day of his death, Joseph was supposed to be taking messages to his brothers at Dothan. But according to the brothers he never turned up. All they found of him was his bloodstained coat.

"He was so proud of that coat," said a witness. "Now it's a coat of many colours with extra red."

Are You-dah Father?

Judah Fathers His Own Grandson

A Canaanite woman disguised herself as a prostitute in order to give birth to an heir. And what is more, the man who slept with her was her father-in-law!

The evidence came out at a sensational trial, where she had been sentenced to death.

Instead, her lawyers produced Judah's seal and staff, which she claimed were given to her as payment when he slept with her. Judah (55) admitted this was true.

"I didn't recognize her at the time, as she was wearing a veil," he admitted. "And anyway it was dark in that olive grove."

Prostitute

Posing as a prostitute, Tamar (24) waited for her recently widowed father-in-law, Judah, as he passed by on the way to shear his sheep.

"She waited by the side of the road," said one witness. "Giving an entirely new meaning to the phrase 'service station'."

When Judah passed by he was unable to resist the temptation, and he slept with her. He even left his seal and staff as a guarantee of payment.

Sensation

When a few months later it was discovered that Tamar was pregnant, she was sentenced to death – it being illegal for any widow to commit adultery. But at that point, she produced her sensational evidence revealing Judah as the father.

"It is not hard to understand why she did what she did," said a friend. "The other brothers were not providing her with the heir she needed. She took action. We may not condone her methods, we may find them hard to understand, but she saw her duty as the continuation of the line. Who knows how God will use her children?"

Brothers Must "Do Their Duty"

Weird Deaths Of Elder Sons

This weird situation is the result of tribal customs that are meant to provide for the continuation of the male line.

Tamar's husband, Er, was Judah's eldest son. After his mysterious death, it was expected that his brother, Onan, would provide his sister-in-law with an heir.

"It is our custom that if an elder brother dies before his wife has conceived, then it is down to the next brother to ... er ... well, 'do his duty' as it were," confirmed a legal expert. "The idea is to provide that woman with a child to continue her line.

"Onan, however, realized that if Tamar had a son, then he and his heirs would get less of the estate. So, although he slept with Tamar, he refrained from the full monty, as it were."

Onan Death

The clan was thrown into consternation when Onan, too, died.

"By custom, Judah's third son, Shelah, should have taken up the task but he is only a young boy. And in any case, I think Judah was getting anxious about these deaths. It seemed like everyone who slept with Tamar kicked the bucket."

Seal And Staff: Police Warning

Police have warned against leaving your seal and staff with any trader, prostitutes, or otherwise.

"Your seal is the symbol of your identity," said a Chief Inspector. "If you give it away anyone could sign agreements or witness contracts in your name.

"Always keep your seal with you, and never tell anyone your PIN."

SEX SLAVE!

Harassment Claim By Wife Of Commander

Potiphar's wife has been attacked by a sex-mad slave! The slave, who goes by the name of Joseph, came to Egypt several years ago, where he was bought by Potiphar in a sale.

"I'm devastated," said the ashen-faced commander. "I thought he was different. I trusted him with everything in my house – all my possessions and all the running of the household. When I told him to relieve me of my responsibilities, I never dreamt he'd take the job so seriously."

Demands

According to Potiphar's wife, Joseph burst in, demanding sex.

"I screamed," sobbed a distraught Mrs Potiphar (24, or so she claims). "Admittedly, not very loudly at first, because I have a cold. Eventually, he fled, leaving only his tunic."

The slave claims he was the subject of advances from his mistress, a story dismissed as a complete fabrication by Potiphar.

"My wife is the purest woman on earth," said the commander. "And anyway, he's just a slave and an Israelite, so we don't have to take any notice of him."

"Liaisons"

According to neighbours, however, Mrs Potiphar has a reputation for extra-marital liaisons.

"I bet the slave didn't fancy her. That's why she had him locked up," said one, who didn't wish to be identified. "Frankly, she's a complete trollop."

Dear Dr Osiris
The Scroll's Soothsayer Unravels Your Dreams

Dear Osiris,

I am an ex-butler who was unjustly downsized by Pharaoh. Lately I've been having these dreams where I see a vine with three branches and, on it, three bunches of grapes. In my dream, I pick the bunches and squeeze them into Pharaoh's cup and put the cup into Pharaoh's hand.

What does it mean?
Yours sincerely,
Osenath Klerik
P.S. The resulting wine is a little rough on the nose but has intriguing undertones of crocodile dung.

Dear Osiris,

Up until recently I was chief baker at court. Following a misunderstanding over some croissants I find myself in jail. In my dreams I have three trays on my head full of pastries and tarts and cakes. But the problem is the birds keep pecking them and flying off with them. What do you advise?
Yours hopefully,
Achmed El Kipling
Exceedingly Good Cake-Maker to Pharaoh.

Osiris answers...

After cutting open a chicken and examined the entrails, I have some good news and some bad news.

The bad news is I haven't got a clue what your dreams are about.

The good news is I've just made a rather nice chicken liver paté.

My advice is to ask someone in jail with you. You never know your luck.

DREAM ON!
Sex-offender Pardoned After Solving Pharaoh's Dreams

Pharaoh has appointed an ex-prisoner to be his chancellor of the exchequer, all because of his dreams!

Joseph (30), a Hebrew slave, was whisked from his cell in Egypt's top security prison to interpret Pharaoh's increasingly bizarre dreams.

The slave had spent years in prison after a sex-claim case made by Mrs Potiphar and her husband.

Weird

"Pharaoh had been dreaming really weird stuff," said a government soothsayer. "We thought he had been sniffing that funny Assyrian incense again. Then his butler, who had only just come out of jail himself, told Pharaoh about Joseph."

Pharaoh sent immediately for the ex-slave and told him all about his dreams.

Joseph told him that the dreams were portents of famine in the land. "According to this Hebrew, there will be seven years of economic growth followed by a major famine, a general collapse in the economy and a sharp decline in the price of pyramids," said one leading economist.

"Needless to say we're looking at his prophecies with some scepticism. But Pharaoh believes that he's right."

Strategy

Not only did Joseph interpret the dreams, he also outlined a strategy for Pharaoh to follow.

"I said that Pharaoh should immediately appoint a wise chancellor," said Joseph. "This official will levy an immediate windfall tax on all food grown during these good years. We're going to build up a store to see us through the lean years ahead."

Appointment

Pharaoh was so impressed that he appointed Joseph immediately, giving him a new name – Lord Zaphenath-Paneah. He will also receive the hand of Pharaoh's daughter in marriage, with the rest of her phased in by next year.

"Words cannot express my joy at this new name, and new bride," said Joseph. "No, really they can't."

GOT CHANGE FOR A CAMEL?
New Currency Proposed

One expert predicts that money will be useless in the slump.

"Forget gold," he said. "Only livestock will be of any use to you."

He is proposing a new system based on animals.

"Roughly speaking, one camel will be worth ten sheep. And you get a hundred rabbits to the sheep. It's a perfectly feasible system, although you do need large pockets for the small change."

Inflation

Not only that, but others are predicting rampant inflation.

"It will be difficult to keep control of the money supply," he admitted. "You know what rabbits are like."

CANAAN REFUGEES ACCUSED OF SPYING

Found-Out Famine Family Sent Packing

Ten brothers who came to Egypt seeking supplies have been branded as SPIES by the Chancellor.

"It was clear from the first that the Chancellor had his suspicions," said a spokesman. "It was almost as if he'd seen these people before. I suppose he just knew the type. He accused them of coming to find out the country's weak points."

The brothers, who are reputed to be of the family of Israel, were given supplies but told that there would not be any more unless they returned with their youngest brother, a boy called Benjamin. One of their number, Simeon, has been held as a hostage until the others should return.

Innocent

"We are totally innocent of these charges," said the eldest of the family, Reuben. "I don't know what Zaphenath-Paneah thought he was doing. All we wanted was some food."

Now the nine free brothers have been sent back to Canaan.

"We came to Egypt because we were starving in our country," said Asher, another brother. "We heard that Egypt had been storing grain for years in preparation for this famine. So we came down here to see if we could buy some. We are not spies. We are just hungry."

"The chancellor was clearly upset by this visit," said a spokesman. "In fact he even burst into tears. I've never seen somebody so upset over espionage."

OH BROTHER!

Chancellor Is Revealed As Long Lost Brother

Family Of Jacob On Their Way To Egypt

Massive Reunion Planned

In an amazing twist Lord Zaphenath-Paneah, the High Chancellor of Egypt, has been reunited with his family, including the very brothers who sold him into slavery 30 years ago.

Gradually the story is emerging. When he was a boy, Joseph was set upon by his elder brothers, angered by his arrogance, his uncanny ability to interpret dreams and his appalling fashion sense. He was sold into slavery, becoming Lord Chancellor nearly nine years ago.

Ruses

"It appears that the Lord Joseph recognized his family the moment he saw them," said his spokesman. "Although they didn't recognize him. Hardly surprising really, as the last time they saw him he was seventeen years old and had been thrown down a well."

The story also explains the Chancellor's frequent and sudden mood swings, and his habit of bursting into tears. "He was clearly very moved by it all. We're extremely relieved as we thought he was several slabs short of a pyramid."

Coming To A Pyramid Near You

The Chief Musician, Achmed El-Webba, has started work on a musical based on the story of Joseph's life.

"It's going to be called 'Lord Zaphenath-Paneah and His Incredible Multicoloured Vision-Tunic'," he explained. "I think it's going to be a big hit."

The musical is expected to be a success in the style of his former productions, "The Phantom of the Temple" and "Sungod Boulevard".

Pharaoh In "Nilegate" Land Acquisition Scandal

As the famine in Egypt grows worse, it is expected that most of the land and livestock in the country will pass into Pharaoh's hands. In what the press have dubbed "Nilegate", people are handing over their land in exchange for food.

"We have been buying food from Joseph," said one land-owner, "but now our money has run out. In future, we will have to pay by handing over our live-stock or exchanging our land. We will all end up as smurfs of Pharaoh."

"I think he means 'serfs'," said a friend.

Leased

"No one will be homeless," explained a treasury official. "This is merely an exciting re-financing package which allows the state to take over the land and the landowners to keep breathing. Everyone wins. We think this is a fair and equitable arrangement. But then we're the government, so we would, wouldn't we?"

The Scroll

**24 Sacred Crocodile House
Next to the big Pointy Thing
Valley of the Kings, Egypt**

Jacob Dies

Legendary Leg Puller Fails To Fool Death

More Skeletons In The Closet As Reuben Is Denounced

Jacob, the father of Joseph, is dead.

But not before a final twist in the tail. On his deathbed, Jacob (147) withheld his blessing from his eldest son, Reuben, for committing incest. Many years ago, Reuben slept with one of his father's concubines.

"We all thought the matter was long forgotten," said one brother. "It seems that Father never forgot. That will teach Reuben to practise safe sex."

Scams

Jacob, of course, is no stranger to controversy, especially involving first-born sons. His early life was characterized by a series of cunning and often outrageous scams, which saw him steal his brother's blessing and birthright and build up enormous flocks at the expense of his father-in-law.

"In a way, what he did to Reuben was what he did to Uncle Esau," said another son. "I don't know what he's got against older brothers. Maybe it's some kind of complex."

Israel

Later in his life he was reunited with his brother and returned to Canaan. After a life-changing experience where he claimed to have wrestled with God, Jacob changed his name to Israel.

Even then his life was fraught with difficulties. His daughter was raped and his favourite son, Joseph, was thought to have been killed by a lion. Years later, Joseph turned up in Egypt as Pharaoh's second-in-command.

"It's not exactly been a quiet life," said one friend of the family. "He described his years as 'few and unhappy'."

Jacob is presently being embalmed – a process which is expected to take 40 days. After that he will be buried at Mamre, the burial place of his grand-parents Abraham and Sarah, his parents Isaac and Rebekah and his first wife Leah.

KILL THEM ALL!
Pharaoh Issues Tough New Population Policy

In an attempt to cull the numbers of Israelites in Egypt, all baby boys will be killed.

Following their settlement in Egypt hundreds of years ago, the Israelites grew into a nation within a nation.

Slavery

Pharaoh dealt with the problem by forcing the Israelites into slavery. It was hoped that slum habitation, oppressive working conditions, brutal taskmasters and heavy smoking would cut down their numbers. But the population just kept growing.

Nile

Now Pharaoh has instructed all midwives to kill the Israelite boys.

"All baby boys are to be thrown into the Nile," confirmed the Minister for Culling and General Destruction. "It sounds a bit harsh, but it is important that we take some action. We cannot have these people breeding indefinitely. After all, it's not as if they're important."

Disobey

According to some sources, Israelite women are disobeying the order and finding ways to hide their children.

Princess and the Basket Case
Princess Flaunts New Hebrew Death Guidelines

In direct contradiction to her father's new guidelines, Pharaoh's daughter has adopted a Hebrew boy as her own child.

"I found him floating in a little basket made from reeds," she told a packed press conference. "He was so cute. And anyway, I think Daddy's just being mean over all this."

When challenged on her behaviour, the Princess shouted, "I want him, I want him, I want him!" and held her breath until everybody gave in.

The Princess intends to have the boy raised by a Hebrew nurse.

"I don't want him to completely lose touch with his roots," she said. "In fact, it's quite remarkable how much his new nurse looks like him. But then again, all these Israelites look the same to me."

The boy will be called Moses.

Opposition

Others have opposed the move.

"Once a Hebrew, always a Hebrew," said a constitutional expert. "You wait, that boy will be nothing but trouble."

"You can take the man out of Israel, but you can never take Israel out of the man."

WILL YOU LISTEN TO THAT FLAMIN' BUSH!

Moses Is Back — And This Time It's Personal

"This Bush Spoke To Me" Says Israel's New Spokesman

Moses has returned to Egypt on a mission to liberate his people. And he claims to be powered by God!

"I saw God," he explained. *"I saw a bush that was alive with flame, but which did not burn. A voice spoke to me and told me that he wants the Hebrews to be freed."*

When asked the name of the deity, Moses (80) replied, "He is the God of my ancestors, the God of Abraham, Isaac and Jacob. I asked him his name and he just said, *'I am he who is'."*

Disdain

His message was received with disdain by the authorities.

"An encounter with fiery shrubbery is no basis for executive power," said the Chief Minister, "whether or not it chatted to him. Until he has a mandate from the people, we will ignore him. In fact even if he did have a mandate from the people, we would ignore him. This is a totalitarian regime don't forget."

Unlikely Champion

Moses is an unlikely champion. He has spent many years in the desert as a fugitive from justice. Some see this as a contributory factor in his recent outbursts.

Now aged 80, and with a bad stutter, Moses is accompanied by his brother Aaron, who will be his spokesman.

"My brother is not a natural public speaker," explained Aaron (83). "But he is very hairy. And he bears a striking resemblance to Charlton Heston. *Which are all the qualifications you need, really."*

Twice The Workload

Slaves Work Longer Hours

Pharaoh has responded to Moses' claims by doubling the workload of the Hebrew slaves.

"There will be no changes in the number of bricks the Israelites must make," explained Pharaoh. "It's just now they have to gather the basic materials as well."

"This is a tough time for all of us," he said. "We must remain competitive in the pyramid building business.

"We must keep our noses to the grindstone, backs to the wall and shoulders to the wheel. Otherwise we will be wearing our bile ducts on our shoes – know what I mean?"

Snakes Alive!

Moses' Staff Turns Into Snake

In an alarming display of power, Aaron turned Moses' staff into a serpent!

Initially, he was matched by the Egyptian magicians, who performed the same trick. However, Aaron's snake ate theirs up.

"I'm not sure what this is supposed to prove," said a defiant Pharaoh. "All it indicates to me is that they've perfected the knack of conjuring up reptiles."

Moses used the display of power to demand the release of the Israelites. Pharaoh refused his demands.

"Of course we can't free the Israelites," he said. "But in the meantime, if I want a very fat python I know who to ask."

The Scroll Classifieds

RIVER OF BLOOD

Nile Turns To Blood In New Terrorist Outrage

Moses launched a campaign of terror today, when he turned the River Nile, and all the linked reservoirs, into BLOOD!

The act marks a new escalation in the campaign to free the Israelites from slavery in Egypt. However, his act was met with typical defiance by the government.

"We do not give into terrorism," said Pharaoh. "Mainly, because I'm more terrible than any terrorist you care to mention. But in this case Moses has done nothing that our own magicians could not do. It's just scare tactics."

Pharaoh witnessed the spectacle, but refused to talk to the Israelites, turning his back on them and walking indoors. However, his refusal to negotiate has met with criticisms from normal Egyptians.

"It's all very well for him to walk away," said one. "He's probably got his own water supply. But what am I supposed to do? You can't drink this water. It's filthy and it stinks."

Another said: *"We pay good money for this water. I expect a significant rebate on my water bill.*

"I blame privatization."

Hop it, Moses!

Frogs And Insects Attack

Following the attack on the water supplies, Egypt has been hit by plagues.

First, frogs swarmed out of the river and infested the houses. The frogs were followed by dense clouds of mosquitoes and then by horseflies.

"It's appalling," said a Nile resident. "There are insects in clothes, on the food, on the table, everywhere you go. It's like Scotland in high season."

Battle

The plagues are the work of Moses and Aaron.

"When we set the frogs on you, Pharaoh agreed to our demands," reported Aaron. "So we asked God to kill all the frogs. Immediately we had done this, Pharaoh changed his mind. We had no choice but to send for the mosquitoes."

God

"This is the finger of God," said an Egyptian magician. "Look at the place. Insects everywhere and piles of dead frogs on every street corner. What can you do with them? Someone suggested cooking the legs, but we've not sunk that low."

Meanwhile a spokesman for Insectokill™, Egypt's leading brand of insect repellent, reported that business was booming.

"It's an ill wind, you know..." said a company director. *"Lucky we were privatized just before this."*

FINAL DEMAND

Let Us Go, Or Face The Consequences Warns Moses

The disasters that have struck Egypt during past weeks are nothing compared to what lies in store.

That's the stark warning from Moses and Aaron, unless Pharaoh capitulates to their demands.

"We are tired of Pharaoh's trickery and deceit," thundered Moses. "God is saving the worst till last."

Pharaoh is defiant.

"I will not capitulate," he said. "I have never capitulated. At least, not since I was a baby."

Successive plagues have seen mass outbreaks of boils on people's skin, widespread death of Egyptian livestock and a ferocious spell of thunder, hail and lightning, which decimated the crops.

"Egypt is facing complete ruin," warned one economist. "Our livestock is dead, our flax and barley have been destroyed."

Locusts

As if that wasn't bad enough, the swarm of locusts which hit the country last week is reported to have stripped all the fruit from the branches.

"It's a complete disaster," said a farmer. "I don't know why Pharaoh keeps stonewalling. What is the point of having slaves if the entire country is a barren wasteland?"

Agreement

Other sources reveal that Pharaoh is close to caving in.

He agreed that the Israelites could go and worship God in the desert, but refused when it was apparent that they wanted to take their wives and children as well.

"The original request was for the men to go and sacrifice to God in the desert," said a government official. "Now it appears they will not be happy until all the slaves – men, women and children – are allowed to leave."

"We never said anything about just the men," said Aaron. "God is saying, 'Let my people go and worship me in the desert.' Call me 'Mr Picky', but I reckon 'people' includes men and women."

Darkness

Moses has warned that the next plague – the ninth in this grim catalogue – will plunge Egypt into darkness for three days.

"A power cut – just what we needed," said a disgruntled farmer. *"I bet there won't be a reduction on my candle bill.*

"I blame privatization."

THE DEAD OF THE NIGHT

Night Of Terror Leaves first-born Dead

Families Destroyed By Final Plague

Pharaoh Gives In, As His Heir Lies Dead

The children are dead.

In the middle of the night, the Egyptian firstborn were taken, leaving families numb with grief and despair.

Pharaoh's repeated refusal to allow the Israelites their freedom has led to the most terrible outcome: the death of the firstborn children of Egypt.

No Egyptian family was untouched. Pharaoh lost his eldest son. Lowly prisoners in the city dungeons heard the news of their child's death. Even cattle and livestock lost their babies.

Release

Stunned by the scale of the loss, Pharaoh has announced that the Israelites are free to go, with immediate effect.

He summoned Moses and Aaron to the palace in the early hours of the morning and told them to leave as soon as possible. Egyptians everywhere helped the Israelites on their way, only too pleased to be free at last from the horror of the plagues.

"To lose your eldest child is a terrible tragedy," said a distraught mother. "We did exactly the same thing to the Israelites all those years ago. Now, perhaps we begin to know how they feel."

Special Feast

While Egyptian families were suffering, Israelite families were protected.

Their houses daubed with lamb's blood on the doorpost, the families stayed safe, while the angel of God wreaked havoc in Egypt.

"We will never forget this night," said Moses. "We will always hold a feast to commemorate it."

The feast has been named "Passover" commemorating the fact that God passed over the houses of the Israelites.

GOTCHA!

Pharaoh's Chariots Drowned In Disaster

Moses Opens New Reed Sea By-Pass – And Then Closes It Again

Pharaoh's army were all but destroyed yesterday, after chasing the Israelites into the Sea of Reeds.

The Egyptian monarch had yet another change of heart after releasing the Israelites and chased them by chariot.

However, the pursuit ended in disaster, when Moses destroyed the army by drowning them.

"It was chaos," said one survivor. "No one even thought to bring their swimming trunks, let alone sub-aqua gear."

Trapped

"We thought they were going to be easy pickings," said a survivor. "We had them trapped with their backs to the sea. But then this cloud appeared and this fire, and kept us from attacking them. Not only that but this incredible wind sprang up."

The wind pushed back the waters of the sea, allowing the Israelites to walk through.

"There was this wall of water on each side of them. It was like a huge alleyway through the sea."

Misgivings

Despite the misgivings of his commanders, Pharaoh insisted that his forces pursue the Israelites through the sea.

"It was ridiculous," said one char-ioteer. "Everything was going wrong. The wheels kept falling off the chariots. We wanted to get away. That's when the disaster happened."

Eye-witness accounts are confused, but it appears that at daybreak, Moses stretched out his hand and the sea flowed back into the channel.

"Our army had no chance. The water fell down onto them on both sides. They drowned like rats."

This disaster is the final blow to a beleaguered Pharaoh.

"He was warned what would happen all along," said one palace official. "Now it's too late. He's lost his crops, his livestock, his army and the Israelites. It's not been his best year."

After 430 Years, The Israelites Leave

After four centuries in Egypt some 600,000 Hebrews marched out of the country.

According to eye-witness accounts, the Israelites are being led on their way by a pillar of cloud during the day and a pillar of fire at night.

"They're obviously not very good at map reading," said a source.

"I don't know why they need the guide. They're only going to Canaan. It's hardly going to take them forty years, is it?"

To The Manna Born

Moses Silences Grumblers With Fantastic New Breakfast Cereal

Moses has silenced the grumblers in the camp, by inventing breakfast cereal.

For the past few days, criticism has been growing that Moses had made no provision for the people he brought out of Egypt.

"We were starving," explained one traveller. "At least in Egypt we had food to eat. We also had fish, cucumbers, melon, onions, leeks and garlic. Mind you, we also had the runs, after all that."

Response

Moses' response was to provide a new food called Manna. The food which appears each morning is collected from the desert floor after the dew has gone.

"Just one helping a day provides all the body needs in the form of carbohydrates and roughage," said one expert, "It resembles coriander seeds and has a pleasant honey flavour. I'm not sure, but I think Moses has invented breakfast cereal."

Not only that, but the Israelites have been given meat as well. Last night, a huge flock of quail flew over the camp allowing the hunters to capture and kill as many as they wanted.

Moses Finds Water

There has been quarrelling from the Israelites, as water grows scarce.

Only a few days into their escape from Egypt, the clan have been moaning about the supplies.

"I don't know why we came," said one family. "We seem to have escaped Egypt, only to die of thirst in the desert."

Stoning

Things got so heated in the camp, that the people were almost ready to stone Moses to death.

"I think they would have done it," said one source, "except this being the desert there aren't any stones. It takes a long time to beat someone to death with sand."

Moses' response to the problem was to strike a rock with his staff. The rock immediately burst open and started gushing water. Even then not everyone was impressed.

"The drinking water is OK, but where's the jacuzzi?" said one.

"These people had better watch out," said Moses. "If they carry on moaning, this trip could take years."

New Management Structure

In response to high levels of stress, Moses set up a new management structure.

Following advice from Jethro, his father-in-law, he has appointed judges to oversee sections of the Israelites.

"It was becoming ludicrous. Every dispute was being brought to Moses to decide. Now he can concentrate on only the difficult cases."

Not everyone was so enthusiastic.

"That's the problem with this exodus," grumbled one Israelite. "Too many middle managers."

IS THAT MY DONKEY YOU'RE COVETING?

Adultery Out As Moses Gets Commandments

The first outcome of Moses' meeting with God on Sinai has been revealed.

In a news release issued yesterday, 10 commandments have been laid down by the Lord.

The commandments include prohibitions on idol worship, lying, adultery, coveting other peoples' possessions and even being disrespectful to your parents.

"I'm not sure how I'm going to manage with that one," said one teenager.

System

The commandments are part of a tough new system of laws that God has laid down to guide Israel.

"There will be a lot more detail," confirmed Moses, after his first trip up the mountain. "But these will form the basis for all future laws."

Having delivered these laws, Moses returned to the cloud for more instructions.

Those Rules In Full

- No other Gods but God
- Do not make idols
- Do not misuse the name of God by swearing
- No work on the Sabbath
- Honour father and mother
- No murder
- Or Adultery...
- Or theft...
- No lying
- Do not covet your neighbour's possessions – including his donkey and his wife (although not necessarily in that order)

What you think should have been included

The Scroll's exclusive poll reveals that some key commandments were omitted. Here's what the Israelite in the wilderness wants to add:

- No VAT on straw
- No soggy chips
- No running in the corridors
- No way José
- No through road
- No single currency in the lifetime of this Exodus
- No more opinion polls

OK By Me

Commandments "Generally Acceptable"

Leading lawyers and moral philosophers have agreed that the commandments form a sound basis for future societies.

"I think they are pretty thorough," said one. "Although I would have liked to see 'No Smoking' included."

"I think banning swearing is a ***ing good idea," said another. "I hate those ***ers who do that."

ALL BOW TO THE COW!

Aaron Makes A New God As Israelites Catch Mad Cow Disease

In direct defiance of God's instructions, the Israelites have started worshipping a cow!

The image has been created by none other than the high priest, Aaron.

"Moses has been up that mountain for a long time," explained one worshipper of the golden calf. "So we persuaded Aaron to make new gods for us to worship."

It is not known if the new god has a name, although some have suggested "Daisy" or "Buttercup".

"I don't think that's a very god-like name," said one. "How about 'Oxo' or 'Bovril'?"

Mad

Others, however, condemned the move.

"I can't believe it," said one. "We've not long been out of Egypt and despite all that God has done for us, we are worshipping a golden calf. Somehow, I don't think Moses is going to be too pleased about this. Never mind God."

Experts have even coined a new term for the madness, which has led to scenes of uncontrolled revelry and large-scale sacrifice before the image.

"We call it 'Bovine Sacrifice Epidemic'. Or BSE for short."

KEEP ON TAKING THE TABLETS

Moses Smashes Law Stones

Moses returned from the mount and SMASHED the stones on which God had inscribed the new laws.

These sacred relics were thrown down at the foot of the mountain when he saw the sin the people had committed in front of the cow.

Then Moses ground the calf to dust, scattered the gold on water and forced all the people to drink it.

"I've heard of eating your words, but this is ridiculous," said one ex-calf worshipper.

Riot

By this time people were rioting.

"They were running wild," said one witness, "Moses had no choice but to send troops to restore order."

A squad of crack soldiers from the priestly clan of Levi were sent into the camp to deal with the rioters. Unconfirmed reports indicate some 3,000 have died.

"I don't call that very priestly behaviour," said one calf worshipper, shortly before being "blessed" by a large machete.

Mercy Mission

"This is an appalling sin," thundered a saddened Moses. "We can only hope that God is merciful."

Moses has indicated that he will return to the mountain today to ask God to stay with the Israelites.

"I don't know why he should," remarked one Levite. "After all, God rescued us from Egypt and the first thing we did was replace him with a cow. Sometimes I think we don't deserve him."

New Tablets

Moses hopes to replace the tablets.

"The law was given to us by God," he confirmed. "It is supposed to keep us holy, to purify us, to make us whole and clean. That's why they're called tablets."

How Now Gold Cow?

Donated Gold Creates Idol

The cow was forged from hundreds of items of jewellery, given away by disillusioned Israelites.

They donated bracelets, bangles, necklaces and ingots to be melted down.

"I donated the gold buckle on my belt," said one man, who was later arrested for indecent exposure.

"I threw my gold necklace into the furnace," claimed one young boy. "Well, it was my Mum's really. I just got a bit carried away."

He has been grounded for the next three decades.

God In A Box
Tablets Stored In New "Ark"
Tabernacle Will Be Place To Meet God

God has given new tablets to Moses, to replace the ones smashed in the BSE epidemic.

The tablets given to Moses will be stored in a special box.

Called "The Ark of the Covenant", the box will be housed in the Tabernacle, or Tent of Meeting.

"The Tent of Meeting will be the place where we will meet with God," confirmed Aaron. "I ought to point out that God does not dwell here. We meet him by appointment."

At first people thought that this meant they could take a ticket and wait to be served, but it soon became clear that only certain people would get to meet God.

"Look, this is the Lord, the creator of all things, we are talking about here," said Aaron. "It's not like visiting the dentist, you know."

"Still, it would be nice if they provided a few magazines while we wait," said an Israelite. "And maybe had some music playing or something."

You're Looking Radiant Tonight, Moses
Encounter Gives Him "God Burn"

After encountering God and receiving a new set of stone tablets, Moses' latest encounter left him looking "radiant".

"His face was glowing," said one Levite. "It hurt to look at it. I mean, he's never exactly been an oil-painting, but after meeting with God he looks aglow."

The glow is so extreme that Moses has been forced to wear a veil and shield his face from the Israelites.

"I insisted that he wore a high-factor anointing oil before going up the mountain," said his sister Miriam.

"But no one can go that close to God and not get burned."

It'll Be All White On The Night
Moses' Sister In Leprosy Scare

Miriam, Moses' sister, has been afflicted with leprosy following criticisms of her brother.

The criticisms centred on Moses' marriage and his role as God's spokesman.

"Miriam and Aaron went to the Tent of Meeting and started moaning," said a witness. "They wanted acknowledgement that God also spoke through them. I answered that Moses is a humble man, the most humble man on earth."

"That's typical," said Miriam. "He has to be more humble than anyone else. Talk about big-headed."

Summons

When the Lord heard about this grumbling he descended around them like a cloud. When the cloud departed Miriam was white as snow. She had been infected with leprosy. Her brother prayed for her and God promised her she would be cured. But in the meantime she has had to leave the camp and stay outside.

"She went as white as a sheet," said an eye-witness. "At first I thought it was the world's worst case of dandruff. It was only later we found out it was leprosy."

Coming Next Week...

An extra-special supplement from *The Scroll*

YOUR GUIDE TO THE LEVITICAL LAWS

In association with *Which Sacrifice?* magazine

Look At All These Great Features!

Confused by the new laws?
Don't know which sacrifice is right for you?
Don't know your urim from your thumim?
Unsure what you can eat and when?

You need The Scroll's Guide to the Law
Fully updated for the new Levitical year

Basic Commands

- The Ten Commandments – a user's guide
- Understanding the Wave Offering
- How to get better value out of your sacrifices
- Post-natal cleansing rituals
- The Stain-buster's guide to purifying skin diseases
- Mildew – isolate it and pray it out!

Your Guide To Sacrifices

The Burnt Offering

Hints and tips on Safety, plus special offers on barbecue equipment

The Grain Offering

Seven great cakes for you to sacrifice

The Fellowship Offering

How to check your goat for defects

The Sin Offering

Which animal is right for you?

The Guilt Offering

Tax-efficient ways to pay that 20% levy

Calling all Levites! Levitical Law Pro™

The Scroll's Guide For All Priests

Covers all aspects of professional priestly conduct including:

- Head Shaving
- Behaviour of your Family
- Avoiding Ceremonial Uncleanliness
- Calendar and checklists of Major Feasts and Festivals
- Advice for all Applicants on How to Check themselves for Physical Defect (includes Free Mirror)
- Best Earplugs for the Feast of Trumpets

Sorry – aren't you my sister's cousin's brother-in-law?

A special insert on all unlawful sexual relations! (Includes family tree and identification guide to farmyard animals.)

Jubilee Special

Possibly the most radical and little known aspect of the new laws is the Jubilee Concept where, every fifty years, all property is to be returned to its original owners.

Other aspects include:

- All slaves freed
- All debts written off
- A year spent doing nothing but worshipping God
- No interest charges

This radical social policy needs careful interpretation, and much expert advice if you're to avoid it.

In *The Scroll's* Complete Guide accountants, lawyers, slave salesman and credit agencies will show you the loopholes so that you can keep everything you own.

Hey – Don't Eat that Lizard!

A complete guide to clean and unclean – with pictures and full calorie chart.

NO HONEY PLEASE, WE'RE CHICKENS

Israelites Decide Against The Promised Land

After reports from their spies, the Israelite people have decided AGAINST entering the promised land.

Only two spies – Caleb (45) and Joshua (36) – argued that the land could be taken. All the rest CHICKENED OUT!

The spies were sent in by Moses to check out the land that God had led them to. But when they saw the size of the inhabitants, they decided against invasion.

"They were giants!" said Gaddiel, son of Sodi. "They live in these enormous fortified towns. Even their fruit is bigger than ours. You should see the size of their plums."

Caleb

Only Joshua and Caleb spoke up for the invasion.

"If God has brought us here then we should invade," they said. "This is a land flowing with milk and honey. Well, not literally flowing – that would make everything a bit sticky – but you get the idea."

But others booed them and shouted them down.

"Who wants milk and honey all the time anyway?" said one listener. "I mean, there's only so much honey-flavoured yoghurt you can eat."

Grasshoppers

"They are optimistic fools," said another spy, Ammiel. "We were like grasshoppers next to these people. In fact, I don't even think they were people. I think they were a race of giants from the early time."

Ammiel is on medication.

Forty years on

God Decrees Forty Years More Wandering For Israelites

After their refusal to enter the promised land, God has sentenced the Israelites to wander in the desert for forty years!

"It was only forty days ago that the spies went into the land," said one Israelite. "Now, because we didn't have faith in God we will not be allowed to enter it."

Faith

Now God has decreed that the Israelites will spend the next four decades in the desert, tending their sheep. And of the generation that left Egypt only Caleb and Joshua will be allowed to enter the land. As one tribesman put it:

"We could have had milk and honey, but now we've got sand and sheep-dip."

Wisdom from the Wise

Your questions answered by Bernice, the Wise Woman of Tekoa

Dear Wise Woman,

I'm worried about my son Benjamin. He's getting increasingly hairy and is off his food. I think he may be a Nazirite. How can I tell?

Yours,
Worried of Tent 114

Dear Worried

Don't fret! Becoming a Nazirite is nothing to be ashamed of. In fact, some parents even welcome the change. The best thing is to test early, while the novice Nazirite is preparing for his vows. Here are some tests.

1) Try offering him anything made from grapes. (Don't just stick with wine as he might just be teetotal.) Try offering him raisins or vinegar on his chips. All Nazirites have vowed not to touch any product of the vine.

2) Ask if you can cut his hair. If he says, "No, I have vowed to grow it during my period of separation," you can tell he's a Nazirite.

3) If you have a dead relative handy (or even if your mother doesn't move around much) try getting him to sit next to them. During their period of preparation, Nazirites are forbidden to go near dead people. Or insurance salesmen.

4) Set fire to the tent and shout "women and Nazirites first!" If he runs out ahead of you he may well have taken his vows.

All the best
Bernice

SCROLL SPORTS

All the Action All the Time

AMORITE BEES STING ISRAELITES

**Israelites 0
Amorites 5**

Already banished from the Premier Land for forty years, the Israelites hoped to bounce back with a victory yesterday.

Instead, the fight ended in disaster, with the Israelites soundly defeated by the Amorites.

"We were warned by God that we could not win, but we thought we might get a result out of this one," said an Israeli striker. "Instead, they swarmed all over us like bees. Big bees. Bees with swords."

Now the Israelites have been forced back into the desert to continue their wanderings.

"We rejected the honey and then we got stung," said one supporter.

FULL WEEKEND RESULTS

Canaanites (2) **3**   **Edomites** (0) **0**
Ahiman 28
Sheshai 33
Talmai 78

Amorites (3)**5**   **Israelites** (0) **0**
Sihon, S. 19, 24,
Sihon, T. 35
Sihon, R. 56
Sihon, Maj. Gen. H. J. (Mrs) 68
(Ammiel sent off for failing a
drugs test)

Moabites (4) **5**   **Ammonites** (3) **4**
Eglon 14, 15   Hanun 23, 26, 34
Egroll 17   Lineker 67
Egnog 19
Egg-Foo-Yung 55

Assyrians (3) **3**   **Jebushites** (0) **0**
Tilgash-Pileser 20
Mishmash-Malteser 28
Bigbash-Deepfreeser 36

Egyptians (0) **6**   **Hittites** (6) **6**
Potiphar 46   Uriah 5
Potiplant 49   Gasfiah 8
Potinshed 54   Flatiah 14
Pottiputti 78   Bigliah 27
Potitraining 86 Towncriah 35
Potblack 88   Barbwiah 42

Midianites (3) **4**   **Amalekites** (3) **3**
Zeeb 14   Agag 23
Zebah 17   Agog 37
Zebra 19   Abag 45
Zippadedoodah 55

Philistines (0) **2**   **Perizzites** (3) **3**
Achish 18   Blissett 23, 24, 28
Peckish 20

Kennizites (2) **4**   **Sidonians** (1) **5**
Jinnah 12   Ashtoreth 15, 60
Begginnah 14   Thithelthroth 46
Dogsdinnah 54   Hethetheth 75, 80
Evryonesawinnah 77

MOSES RETIRES

Joshua Appointed Successor

At 120, Moses is about to retire from managing the Israelite team.

He will miss out on promotion and will not lead them across the Jordan into the promised land.

For forty years the veteran leader has led the Israelites in the desert. Now he wants to retire and hand over to Joshua (76) for the preparations to finally enter Canaan.

"I'm ready for a rest," he said. "God told me that I would never enter the promised land. I have to accept that."

Joshua paid tribute to his predecessor.

"The Gaffer done great," he said. "He build a solid team, although he was badly let down by some of the squad and never achieved the promotion to the Premiership that he so richly deserved."

Of his own appointment, Joshua said, "I'm over the moon – or across the Jordan more specifically."

Books

Moses has plenty of plans for the next few months.

"I'm going to write my memoirs and the book of law," he said. "The publishers want to call it *Moses – An Old Bloke Who Served God*. Personally I prefer *Exodus*."

Spies Found In Prostitute's House

"We Were Hiding From The Enemy," Claim Red-faced Pair

Two spies sent by Joshua ahead of the invasion force have been saved by hiding in a brothel!

The spies were sent into Jericho to help Joshua plan the campaign against the city. The first thing they did was to set up their base in a brothel.

"It was a strategic move," said one of the spies. "Honest."

Rescue

When the authorities became suspicious, orders were given to search the house. But the two men were hidden by the prostitute, who was called Rahab.

Stories

"Everyone has heard about how God rescued the Israelites," said Rahab (25). "Everyone in the city is scared of them. I was simply doing a deal and saving the life of my family."

The spies were hidden under a pile of drying straw on the roof, before making their escape down ropes. Since the house is built into the city wall, they were then able to cross the five miles to the Jordan and report back to base.

ATISHOO! ATISHOO! WALL FALL DOWN!

Jericho Surrenders To Israeli Noise

Insurers Refuse Pay Out On Wall Collapse

Jericho has been conquered. In a spectacular display of power, the walls of the city collapsed, leaving the inhabitants defenceless and allowing the Israelites to take the city.

For seven days the Israelites have marched around the city, doing nothing but playing their trumpets.

"It was becoming a bit tedious to be honest," said one marcher. "I mean, I like a brass band as much as the next man, but seven days is more than enough."

Cont. on page 53

The process was part of a cunning plan to demoralize the inhabitants of the city and lower their defences.

"It was a kind of noise torture, I suppose. Especially given the lack of technique some of our trumpeters have."

"It was psychological warfare," another commented. "I thought the performance of the hits of Showaddywaddy was a masterstroke."

Shout

At the end of the seven days, the army gave a huge shout and the walls of Jericho collapsed.

"It was like an earthquake," said one witness. "The walls just folded outwards and we rushed in through the gaps. They never stood a chance."

Burnt

Now the city has been put to the torch and all the inhabitants destroyed.

"We killed everybody," said a soldier. "Men, women, donkeys, cattle, hamsters, every living thing. Those were our instructions. And after they had to listen to seven days of that trumpet playing, it was more of a mercy killing than anything else."

'Ai' Feel Really Stupid

City Destroyed By Simple Ruse

SCROLL SPORTS

The Israelites scored a decisive victory in the Canaan Conquest Cup when they destroyed the city of Ai by pretending to run away.

"We'd worked our game plan out pretty carefully," said one soldier. "The idea was to attack, then withdraw, then hit them on the break."

Shortly after attacking the city, the Israelites turned and ran. The opposition, thinking the Israelites to be beaten, stormed out and followed them. No sooner had they disappeared, than a secondary force, who had been hiding, ran out, nipped into the city and started burning.

Shocking

"It was a shocking defensive error," admitted the Ai manager. "We thought we had them on the run, so we forgot to leave anyone at the back. We normally play a sweeper system, but he'd lost his spear, so he was useless."

Following this defeat, there have been calls for the Ai manager to resign, but these have been rejected on the grounds that he has just been hanged. "I think that could be taken as dismissal," said one employment expert.

Delighted

"We were delighted with the way the battle went," said Joshua (77). "The only problem with the plan was finding the city in the first place. When we asked people what city lay in the distance they kept saying 'Ai'. I thought they were all deaf. It took me ages to realize we were on the right road."

Insurers Refuse Payouts

Meanwhile insurance companies have refused to pay out on the grounds that "aggressive trumpet playing" is not covered.

"We don't cover against acts of war, or very loud trumpet playing, which amounts to much the same thing," said a spokesman.

"Anyway, since most of the inhabitants of Jericho are dead, I doubt they'll be in much of a position to fill in their claims forms."

Jericho: The Tribute Album

Some of the trumpeters involved in this victory for loud honking wind instruments, are to record a tribute album. Some of the tracks include:

• Wall Meet Again

• Round and Round

• Shaking Wall Over

• Should I Stay or Should I Blow

• No Shout About It

Joshua Dies Aged 110

Joshua is dead. He has been buried on his estate in the highlands of Ephraim.

"He led us into the promised land," said one fan. "He was a great manager. Some of his tactics, like the pretend retreat and the full-on trumpet attack were magnificent.

"Now we must look to the future. As long as we stick to the laws of God we should be OK. But then again, we're not particularly good at doing that, are we?"

OVER THE HILT AND FAR AWAY!

Massive Moabite Monarch Is Murdered

Assassin Escapes As Aides Wait For King To Relieve Himself

King Eglon, the fat monarch of Moab, has been murdered by an assassin. So fat was the king that his stomach closed over the hilt of the sword, meaning the assassin had to leave it behind.

The murder was not discovered for several hours, allowing the assassin to make good his escape. "We thought the King was on the toilet," explained a palace aide. "It's not unusual for him to spend several hours on the throne. He is a king after all."

Ehud

The King (52) was killed yesterday, after a visit from Ehud (28), the son of Gera. Ehud had come from the Israelites with an annual payment to the man who had conquered their country.

"After the payment was delivered, Ehud requested some time alone with the King," said an informed source. "He said he had a special message for Eglon from God. Obviously the message had a point to it."

Left-handed Man

Police are refusing to confirm or deny that they are searching for Ehud. However, they have revealed that the murder

Cont. on page 55

was committed by a "left-handed man". Ehud is known to be left-handed, despite the fact that he comes from the tribe of Benjamin, which literally means "son of my right hand".

"The murder was committed yesterday, while the King was in private audience," said a police-man. "The murder weapon must have been smuggled in under the assassin's clothing."

Fat

Police sources confirmed that the weapon went right through the King's body and out the back, with the King's fat stom-ach closing over the hilt. The murderer escaped through the porch, closing and locking the door behind him.

"We have checked the sword for prints, but most of them were wiped off by the King's stom-ach," said the Inspector heading up the case. "And there's not much point dusting for fat."

Turmoil

This murder has thrown into tur-moil the government of Moab. What is more, latest reports indi-cate that Ehud has escaped across the river and is even now massing a force to attack.

Eglon himself will not be remembered with any fondness.

"He's become a bit of a joke really," said one citizen. "I sup-pose he'll be remembered as the King who put the 'die' in 'diet'."

Do You Know This Man?

Young, left-handed, possibly with a greasy sort of stain on his tunic.

If you recognize this desciption, please contact the Moabite Police, Big Fat Dead Body Department.

THE SCROLL SAYS

Eglon Their Faces

Eglon is dead. Good riddance, we say.

But the truth is he should never have conquered Canaan in the first place.

If the Israelites had followed God they would not have been enslaved by a man who made the speak-your-weight machine go "ouch". They would have run their own country.

Instead they forgot their history and were left with egg on their faces.

The Israelites have forgotten God. Each man does what he thinks fit.

Is that any way to run a country?

The Scroll says, "Pull Yourself Together Israel!"

How Fat Was Eglon?

HERE ARE THE FACTS:

• Ehud's sword was 18 inches long.
• The tip of the blade came out the back of the King's body, while his fat closed over the hilt
• This means that the King was at least 18 inches in diameter.

A mathematician writes: *"Using simple maths, we can calcu-late that he had a waist measurement of 56 inches! This would explain why his aides were so used to him spending a long time on the loo. When you're nearly five foot round, it's hard to get up quickly. Whatever the case, it has clearly been many years since he last saw his knees!"*

Sisera Pegs Out
Woman Takes Monarch Down A Peg Or Two

Sisera, the commander of the Canaanites has been killed — with a tent peg!

His assassin, a woman called Jael, drove the peg through his head while he took shelter in his tent.

"It might seem grisly to some people," she admitted. "But it was nothing to changing nappies."

Sisera was in retreat, after his forces were beaten by the Israelites.

"I wasn't sure who he was at first," said Jael (23). "He was all hot and sweaty and covered in blood from the battle. But I knew he was a general when I saw his pips. I invited him into my tent and gave him some milk. He said if anyone came asking after him he wasn't there."

Mallet

While Sisera drank his pinta, Jael grabbed a mallet and a few moments later, Sisera was doing his impression of a groundsheet.

Barak (58), the leader of the Israelites, found the body when he rode up to the tent in pursuit.

"That's what I call a splitting headache," said Barak. "I realized straight away that Sisera was beyond the powers of Aspirin. It was a good thing for us that Sisera went straight to Jael. He did not pass go. He will not collect two hundred pounds."

Wisdom from the Wise
Bernice, the Wise Woman of Tekoa, Answers Your Questions

Dear Wise Woman,

I am a wife and mother living in a tent near Zaanannim. Following an incident yesterday, there is a lot of blood on my carpets. Not to mention bits of brain and the odd fragment of skull. Any advice on how to remove these stains?

Yours, 'J'.

P.S. I'm telling the neighbours it was a camping accident.

Bernice writes...

Wise up girl! Cleaning is for wimps. We're power-women now so just get out and BUY a new carpet. You're a heroine for heaven's sake. Make the most of it. And while you're at it, move to a place with less Zs and As in the title. It sounds like the kind of noise a camel makes after eating a particularly hot thistle.

Deborah – An Inspiration To Us All

Credit for Jael's action must go to Deborah, the prophetess who is judge over all Israelites at the moment.

"She's a bit of a role model," confessed one Israelite woman. "It's good for the country to have a strong woman in charge."

Deborah (75 if she's a day) revealed that Jael succeeded because Barak, the Israelite commander, failed.

"It's true that Barak went and attacked the Canaanite army when I told him. However, he wanted me to go along with him. Typical men. Can't do a simple thing like destroy an enemy army without someone holding their hand.

"It only goes to show the truth of that saying: 'Behind every great man there's a very surprised woman'."

Glory

Deborah decreed that because she had to accompany him, Barak would not get the honour of defeating the general.

"I knew then that the glory of this day would go to a woman."

Barak, however, was unrepentant.

"Oh yeah, like I mind," he said. "It's fine by me if someone else wants to drive a peg through this bloke's bonce. I saved a fortune on the dry-cleaning bills."

GIDE-ON MY SON!

Army Facing Massive Redundancies

Gideon (36) has been preparing for the offensive against the Midianites by SACKING most of his army.

"He seems to believe that if you have a big army it takes too much credit from God," said one ex-paratrooper. "So he's been using more and more bizarre ways to cut down the numbers."

Scared

Gideon's first ploy was simply to send home anyone who was scared.

"Anyone who was trembling was allowed to take the day off and watch the battle from Mount Gilboa," said one officer. "They didn't even have to bring a note from their mums."

The next selection procedure was based on drinking practices.

"At first we thought it was all about chucking out anyone who had too much alcohol last night," said a squaddie. "We were a bit worried because that would have left an army of about five people. But it was all about how we drank water."

Lapped

Anyone who lay down and lapped the water made it into the final squad.

Final numbers are unclear, but a vast proportion of the army will not take part.

"It's getting stupid," said one reservist. "He's only got three hundred left. And one of them is the regimental goat."

Gideon Beats Midian

Troops Go "Potty" In Night

Regimental Goat Badly Wounded

In a surprise attack, Gideon's three hundred troops have routed the Midianite forces.

Using a variation on the famous "Jericho manoeuvre", Gideon's men surrounded the camp around midnight. Each man was armed mainly with a pot, a trumpet and a torch.

At Gideon's signal the men SMASHED their pots, BLEW their trumpets and SHOUTED at the enemy.

The enemy, who were thrown into total confusion, fled in every direction, setting fire to their tents and even killing each other in the stampede.

Panic

"There was total panic," confirmed one soldier. "The sound of all that breaking crockery seemed to completely unnerve them. Maybe they're all porcelain collectors or something."

There were no Israelite casualties, with the exception of the regimental goat (6), who cut his hoof on a piece of broken pot.

"Naturally we're worried about Billy," said his handler. "But if he doesn't pull through at least we can make a nice curry."

NIGHT OF THE FOX

Lovers' Tiff Sets Fields On Fire

Israelite Hero Destroys Philistine crops

Samson, the Israelite strongman, has single-handedly destroyed the Philistine harvest after he was jilted by his bride.

The Israelite hero had intended to visit his Philistine wife, when he discovered that she had been given to someone else.

"He was such a long time between visits," explained his father-in-law. "I thought he'd gone off with someone else. So I gave her to one of his friends. I don't know what he's complaining about. I offered him her sister."

Samson (28) took his revenge by capturing 300 foxes, tying burning torches to their tails and setting them free to run through the Philistine fields and vineyards. In the ensuing havoc, all the Philistine crops were ruined.

"I understand he was upset," said the girl's father, 'but even so I think he over-reacted. Maybe counselling would have helped."

From Jawbone To War-bone!

Samson Massacres Thousands With A Donkey's Jawbone

**In one corner a hairy Israelite armed with a donkey's jawbone.
In the other one thousand heavily armed Philistines.
The odds: 1,000–1.
THEY NEVER STOOD A CHANCE.**

In one of the most astonishing feats of arms ever witnessed, Samson massacred 1,000 Philistines using only a bit of old donkey.

The Philistines thought they had captured Samson, after he was handed over to them by back-stabbing and cowardly compatriots. The Philistines threatened to make war on the tribe of Judah unless Samson was handed over. Accordingly, Samson agreed to be bound and taken to the Philistines.

Escape

As soon as he got near the enemy, however, he burst his ropes, snatched up the jawbone of a dead donkey and set to work.

"I had to think quickly," he admitted afterwards. "It was a bit of a tricky situation. I could probably have killed them without a weapon, but it would have taken a lot longer. It was just lucky someone had dropped the dead donkey."

HAIR TODAY— GONE TOMOR- ROW!

Shaggy Samson Loses Locks To Lover

The secret of Samson's strength is out, as his lover Delilah cut him off in his prime.

She shaved off his hair, leaving the Israelite strongman as weak as a baby.

"I was a fool," said Samson. "I loved her. But that's women for you. You think you can trust them and they go and shave your barnet."

Nagging

For some time, Delilah (18) had been trying to find out the secret of Samson's astonishing strength. She had been promised a large sum of money by the Philistines if she would deliver the Israelite hero to them.

"In the end he grew sick of her nagging," said a servant. "He told her the truth just to keep her quiet."

Blinded

Now Samson has been trussed up and BLINDED by the Philistines.

"He thought he was so high and mighty," they mocked. "Now he's blind and bald."

His fate is uncertain. Last reports seem to indicate that he has been taken to Gaza, where he has been set to work on a treadmill.

"He once slaughtered thousands of men with a donkey's jawbone," said a spokesman. "Now they've really made an ass of him."

SIGHTLESS SAMSON BRINGS THE HOUSE DOWN

Samson Buries Thousands of Pillar-stines!

It was a final act of defiance.

Paraded before the Philistines like a helpless animal, Samson pulled the pillars of the building down, killing himself and everyone inside.

"He may have been blind as a bat, but he was strong as an elephant," said an observer. "A very strong elephant. An elephant on steroids."

Samson was able to perform this last, heroic act of defiance, because the foolish Philistines had let his hair grow again.

Mix-up

"We had booked him in at the hairdresser's for the week before," confessed an embarrassed official. "But there was a bit of a diary mix up. Samson was also scheduled to spend most of that morning on the treadmill and the afternoon being laughed at and generally mocked. So we put it off for a week."

"At the banquet, the Philistines were singing the usual triumphant chants," said one onlooker. "You know, 'We Are the Champions', 'One-nil to the Philistines', and 'Who Put Out the Eyes?'. No one noticed that Samson had been led to the pillars which supported the building."

One final push was all it took. Samson had his revenge and his captors were left in the rubble.

WE WANT A KING!

Israelite "Yes" Vote Disappoints God

Israel wants a king. That's the cry from the people after hundreds of years of chaos and anarchy.

"Ever since we entered the promised land, it's been a hideous trauma," said the spokesman for GIMME (Give Israel Many Monarchs Evermore). "We need leadership. Every other country has a king, why can't we?"

"It is obvious from public opinion that the people want a king. The 'judges' who have led us since the time of Gideon are an anachronism. We need a new political system. We need a bloke with big ears who can wander about shaking hands. We need New Monarchy."

Slaves

Meanwhile, Samuel, the prophet, proclaimed that God was against it.

"We should be ruled by God, not by monarchs," he said. "What will a King do? He will simply take your sons for his army and your children to serve in his household. He will take the best of your possessions for himself. You will be little more than slaves. That is what God says."

Many people were surprised at God's opposition.

"Just because God is the ruler of the universe doesn't mean he can't be a republican," said Samuel (78). "He's just being realistic. And since he invented reality he should know what he's talking about."

Corruption

Samuel has been accused of being biased in this matter. He is the last true judge of Israel, but his sons, whom he appointed, have been accused of bribery and corruption.

"It's all very well for Samuel to say that," said one political reformer, "but his sons just illustrate the failure of the judge system. We are determined to have a King so that we can be like everyone else. We want a king to lead us and fight our battles."

Appointment

Despite God's opposition to the plan, Samuel indicated that a King would be appointed.

"He has listened to his people and he will act," said the ancient prophet. "They will get what they want. I hope it's what they thought they wanted."

THAT'S SAUL FOLKS!

Saul Is Appointed King

Donkey Driver Gets Top Job

Saul, a young man from the tribe of Benjamin, has been appointed King by the prophet Samuel. His appointment has been confirmed by the drawing of lots from all the tribes of Israel.

The young man, who only a few days ago was running errands for his father, searching for a load of lost donkeys, is now the monarch of all Israel.

Donkeys

"God told me I would meet a young man from the tribe of Benjamin, looking for his donkeys," said Samuel. "That was the person who would be king. Don't ask me why donkeys are involved. I can only assume it's the Lord's sense of humour."

Saul (20) will now go to Gilgal to offer sacrifices.

"He won't be crowned," said an organizer, "because we haven't got a crown yet. But we've ordered one from 'Tiaras R Us' and as soon as it arrives, we'll slap it on."

Samuel Retires

Last Of The Judges Steps Down From The Bench

Samuel has retired. He has been the chief prophet of Israel since he was only eight.

His last years have been marked by the continuing misbehaviour of his sons and the controversy over the New Monarchy debate.

It was only yesterday that he was calling down thunder and lightning to prove God did not want Israel to have a King.

"Old party tricks do not change the position," said an opponent. "If we listened to everyone who could call down hail and lightning, this country would be ruled by the weathermen."

Retire

"I have made my point," Samuel concluded. "Now we must just get on with it. In the meantime I want to retire without rancour or bitterness.

"So if there is anyone I have wronged, anyone whose ox I have taken, or whose donkey I have pinched, let them speak now or forever hold their peace."

No one spoke. Except for one who muttered, "I wish he'd stop going on about donkeys."

MISHMASH AT MICHMASH

Saul Defeats The Philistines

But Rumours Persist About His Suitability For Job

Saul has capped a great few months with the defeat of the Philistine army.

Despite being holed up in caves and lacking any proper equipment, the Israelites defeated the Philistines in a bloody and confusing battle.

"I'm over the moon," said Saul. "It was touch and go there for a while, but God was with us."

Things did not look good for the Israelites in the battle. When the army was called together it was discovered that only two people had swords.

Blacksmiths

"The Philistines have closed all the blacksmith shops in the country," said an observer. "They controlled the supply of weapons. You couldn't get a sword for love nor money.

"Only Saul and his son had proper weapons. The rest of us had to make do with bits of metal and stones and stuff like that. One bloke brought his saucepan. Not only did he take out three Philistine soldiers with it, he also cooked great fried eggs."

The battle took place in the pass of Michmash and once the Israelites attacked the Philistines panicked.

"There was full-scale chaos there," said one soldier. "People were defecting from one side to the other. In the end, we saw the Philistines running away and we knew we'd won."

Rumours

Despite this victory, rumours persist about Saul's unsuitability for the post. It has been claimed that his son, Jonathan (18), broke the fast which the soldiers had sworn to observe. And many experts believe Saul is falling out of favour with God.

"His trouble is he doesn't obey instructions," said one expert. "He's too headstrong, too wilful, and frankly, too unstable. I can't see him lasting the course."

Replacement

Samuel is even rumoured to be looking for a replacement.

"I don't know where he's looking, but I've heard rumours that Samuel wants to appoint a shepherd in Saul's place," said one source.

"He's obviously going to give sheep a try, now that the donkeys have proved unsuccessful."

SCROLL SPORTS

All the Action All the Time

I'LL KILL YOU ALL!

A *Scroll* Exclusive Interview With Goliath

Interviewed by our single combat correspondent, Harry Ben Carpenter.

Be afraid ... be very afraid. Just when you thought it was safe to go back into the pastures, the Philistines are back. And this time they've got Goliath on their side.

Goliath walked into the room without bothering to open the door. You can hear him coming three miles away. He's nine foot tall, and built like a brick altar. This is the man they call the 'wrath of Gath'. This is Goliath.

The Scroll: **Tell us a bit about yourself.**
Goliath: I'm here to do a job. Saul thinks he's anointed? I'll tell him where to put his ... er... 'nointment.

The Scroll: **You've challenged any Israelite to single combat. What do you think will happen?**
Goliath: I'll kill them all, one by one. But they won't fight me, 'cause they too scared. They just turkey.

The Scroll: **Chicken.**
Goliath: No thanks, I'm not hungry.

The Scroll: **Now some people have said that you're just a bruiser, a big lad with no real technique. What do you say to that?**
Goliath: I say this ... er ....
 He fumbles in his pocket for a piece of paper.
Goliath: "Their champion will fall by the end of round two, I float like a butterfly, sting like a gnu."

The Scroll: **A gnu?**
Goliath: I couldn't think of another rhyme for "two". Anyway, the point is there's a lot more to me than meets the eye. I'm a poet as well as a psychotic killing machine. Although, to be fair, most of my poems are about what it's like being a psychotic killing machine and how much fun it is. Here, I've got another one. It goes, "I wandered lonely as a cloud ... and then I tore someone's head off." I also do abstract art. What I do is rip someone's arm of and then paint using the wet end.

The Scroll: **So, how do you see the battle going?**
Goliath: Ain't no one going to stop me. They're going down, you hear? 'Cos I float like a butterbean, sting like a knee ... oh, no hold on, that's not right...

Goliath may have the muscles of a grizzly bear, but he also has the IQ of a housebrick. Will you tell him, or shall I?

SCROLL SPORTS

All the Action From the Big Fight

The Contenders

Name: Goliath

Nationality: Philistine

Club: Maiming Club of Gath

Age: Not known. You'd have to cut his leg off and count the rings.

Height: Nine feet

Weight: Incalculable

Reach: No one's ever got near enough and survived.

Special Weapon: Spear

Previous Record: Fought 300. Won 300. Killed 300.

Nicknames: "The Wrath of Gath"

Name: David

Nationality: Israelite

Club: Shepherd's & Harpists Affiliated

Age: 17

Height: Small, but could use a ladder if need be.

Weight: Light

Reach: 75 feet using his sling

Special Weapon: Sling and Pebble

Previous Record: Fought 0. Won 0. Killed 0. (Not including lions).

Nicknames: Oi! You Over There!

The Big Fight
What the experts say:

"If I were David, I wouldn't go for any close stuff. His best bet for survival is to keep his distance. About 30 miles should be enough."
Harry Ben Carpenter,
The Scroll **Single Combat Correspondent**

"You've got to admit the lad's got guts. And you've got to believe we'll soon be seeing them."
Henry the Barrelmaker, ex-Champion of All Israel

"I'm offering odds of 5–1 against David, I can't say fairer than that."
"Honest" Ephraim, Bookmaker to the Stars

"I am lovely."
Chris Nilebank

"Not as lovely as me."
"Prince" Hasaam of the Moabites

"All right, 8–1 then. Any takers?"
"Honest" Ephraim, Bookmaker to the Stars

"This promises to be a real thrill-fest for the fight fan. It's got everything – blood, gore, bones snapped like twigs, gouged eyeballs. So grab yourself a beer and enjoy it!"
Israel Women's Weekly

"I admire the lad's spirit. And I commend it to God. I just wish the rest of you were as grateful to have me. I'd fight him myself, only I've got this bad back."
King Saul

"If you'd listened to me we'd never have been in this mess."
Samuel

"250–1, anybody?"
"Honest" Ephraim

"I am still lovely."
Chris Nilebank

SCROLL SPORTS
All the Action All the Time

THE FALL OF A GIANT
Goliath Killed In World Championship Fight

World Champion Goliath was spectacularly defeated yesterday, by a young shepherd boy.

David (17), a shepherd and part-time harpist, accepted the challenge from the nine-foot-tall Philistine, fighting in the colours of Gath.

"I'm very pleased," said David. "In fact the hardest thing about the contest was picking up his sword to hack his head off after he was dead.

"I wasn't afraid. After all, I've fought lions! The trick was to think of him as a big lion, standing up."

"It's amazing," said our single combat correspondent, Harry Ben Carpenter. "We thought Goliath was invincible. I mean, the guy could crack walnuts with his eyelids. Even his muscles had muscles."

Sling

Even more amazing, David went into the fight wearing no armour and carrying nothing more than a sling.

"He'd clearly done his homework," said Harry. "After all, you couldn't hope to slug it out face to face. For a start you'd need a ladder just to see Goliath's face. No, the answer was to be mobile, quick and hit on the run."

Cheese

David was certainly an unexpected contender. He only heard about the fight when he came to the camp to deliver some cheese.

"The Philistines made unsubstantiated drug allegations," confirmed one official, "so we've had the cheese tested. It tasted very nice on a cracker."

Monster

Above all, people are praising David for his heroic faith.

"It took a lot of guts for the boy to go out there and face this monster," Harry said.

"Especially when you consider that Goliath was previously undefeated. I mean, never mind bite somebody's ear – this guy would bite your whole head off. But David never seemed to think he could lose."

How The Fight Was Fought

Round One

(1) Goliath challenges any Israelite to single combat. Nobody volunteers. Goliath wins on points.

Round Two

(2) David volunteers to fight. He tries on Saul's armour but is unable to move. The Philistines are unimpressed.

Round Three

(3) David goes out to meet Goliath armed with only a sling and five pebbles. Goliath mocks the boy and threatens to "give your flesh to the birds and the animals!" Most neutrals have Goliath ahead at this stage.

Round Four

(4) Goliath lumbers to meet the boy. David runs towards him, whirls his sling and fires a pebble right between Goliath's eyes. Two minutes later Goliath's body realizes it is dead.

Round Five

(5) The referee stops the fight on the grounds that Goliath is dead. David cuts his head off just to make sure.

Round Six

(6) The Philistines flee in terror. David declared the champion.

Giant Slayer Tipped As King

"Sky's the limit" say top priests

The sky's the limit for the new champion of Israel, according to priestly sources.

Rumours abound that David has been secretly anointed King by Samuel, in preference to Saul.

When approached on the matter by reporters, Saul threw a spear at them.

Unhappy

A number of high-ranking priests are said to be unhappy with Saul's performance at the dispatch box – or more specifically, dispatching enemies.

"He started very well, with a landslide victory," said one, "but New Monarchy hasn't so far lived up to its promises.

"*We think this David boy has a big future ahead of him.*"

IT'S TIME FOR ME TO DIS-A SPEAR !

David Rebels Against Saul After Spear-throwing Incident

"This Could Mean Civil War"

EXCLUSIVE

David is now officially at war with Saul following the breakdown in relations between them and the increasing paranoia of the King.

In the past few weeks, Saul (45) has become increasingly threatened by David's popularity, even going to the extent of throwing a spear at the boy while he was singing one of his songs.

"We don't like to view it as an act of violence," claimed a Palace spokesman.

"We prefer to think it was a piece of music criticism. Maybe he just wanted a different song. I mean, there are only so many songs about the joys of tending sheep that a monarch wants to hear."

Undermined

Most observers, however, see the split as more fundamental.

Saul has been increasingly undermined by David's success on the field of battle, his victories over the Philistines, the defeat of Goliath and the evident popularity of this young hero.

Now their feud has boiled over into a conflict that could easily lead to civil war. David is in the desert with about six hundred men and is engaged in guerilla warfare against his former King.

"As long as he doesn't sing to us," said a Palace spokesman.

LET OFF ON THE LOO

Saul Has A Close Call Of Nature

"David has Killed His Tens of Thousands"
The Songs That Irritated Saul

One of the key factors in Saul's dislike of David has been the young man's popularity, especially the songs that the troop have been singing about them.

"Saul has killed his thousands, and David his tens of thousands," ran the most popular chant.

Others included:
- "One-nil to the Israelite"
- "Sing when you're slinging, you only sing when you're slinging"
- "Who's that weakling in the crown?"
- "Saul is a bit of a prat quite frankly"

According to the latest reports from the front line, Saul has had a dramatic escape from death.

The King went into a cave to go to the toilet without realizing that David and his men were hiding at the back. According to reports, David crept up while the King was "otherwise engaged" and cut off a corner of his robe.

When the King left the cave and was some distance away, David emerged and shouted to the King about what he'd done.

"He tried to make the King understand that he could have killed him, but didn't," said an official.

Tears

"The King just burst into tears. There is a part of Saul which knows that David is actually a really good man. The trouble is it's not the part of Saul which holds the spear, to coin a phrase."

Nevertheless, they have concluded a temporary truce, allowing Saul to concentrate on the imminent threat of invasion by the Philistines.

Loitering

Others, however, took a less than charitable view.

"If you ask me, you have to wonder what David was doing loitering in a public toilet," said the guardian of the King's Chamberpot, in Jerusalem.

"And as for the King, a damp, cold cave is no place to go to the toilet. You could get piles. Not to mention a spear in the ribs."

WITCH WAY NOW?

Saul Calls In The Spiritualist

Saul, in terror of the imminent Philistine attack, has been consulting a medium.

"She prefers the term 'Spiritual Communications Expert'," said a palace official. "It sounds a bit more professional."

The move can be seen as one more step in Saul's descent. No Israelite leader in the past would have countenanced such a meeting.

"Look, this is the modern world," said Saul's press spokesman. "We have to respect – and learn from – all different traditions." The Witch – to use an old-fashioned term – lives at En-Dor.

Outlawed

"I don't think the meeting went well," said an observer. "For one thing, the woman suspected who he was, and since he'd already passed laws outlawing such practices she naturally feared a trap."

Saul (48) instructed the witch (72) to call up the ghost of Samuel (dead). When the prophet appeared he was, as usual, in a very bad mood.

Grumpy

"He laid into Saul for what he was doing, how evil it was, and how God would now abandon Saul to the Philistines. It was typical Samuel. He was always grumpy when woken up. Doubly so when woken from the dead."

Now Saul must face the Philistines knowing that he has abandoned God and turned to other forces. It remains to be seen whether this new multi-faith approach will work.

SAUL – THE KING'S STORY

THE SCROLL SAYS

He's Losing It

It's not just the war against David.

It's not just the war against the Philistines.

Saul is losing it where it really matters.

Between his ears.

Never the most stable of men, he has long been known to have the temper of a bull hippo with toothache. But this visit to the witch is a new low.

Whatever the events of the next few weeks, one thing is sure.

David has won.

Israel must now face the future.

For too long, Israel's history has been one of death, greed, arrogance, donkeys and despair. And those were the good days.

Now a new era must begin.

The Scroll says, "Let's All Pull Together, Israel!"

SAUL ALONE

King Commits Suicide
Tragic death of failed monarch

In the wake of his disastrous defeat at the hands of the Philistines, Saul has taken his own life.

He was badly wounded in the fighting, which also carried off his son Jonathan, and several of his children. To avoid being taken alive, he fell on his own sword.

His body was originally taken by the Philistines and paraded on the walls of the city of Beth-Shean. It was rescued in a daring night raid by the warriors of Jabesh Gilead.

"We marched through the night and recovered the bodies from the walls, where they had been hung," said one warrior. "Unfortunately the King had been beheaded."

"It seems like even in death he couldn't keep his head."

David Is King
Following the death of Saul, David has been crowned at Hebron.

Although the followers of Saul have lost their King, they are continuing to fight on.

David (30) is thought to be willing to compromise but is insistent on the return of Michal, Saul's daughter and his wife.

"It is only a matter of time before David unifies the nation once again," said his press officer. "He is the man the people want. We have to drive the Philistines out."

KING DAVID AND THE WIFE OF BATH

David Falls For Bathing Beauty

King David has fallen in love with a woman he saw bathing!

According to the latest gossip from the palace, David's new love is a woman he saw from a nearby rooftop.

"You know how these things happen," said a palace insider. "The King just went out to get a breath of fresh air, and happened to glance across to a nearby rooftop. This woman was taking a bath and David fell in love."

He refused to say what attracted the King. "Let's just say it wasn't her rubber duck," he hinted.

Adultery

However, the rumours are that the object of the King's desire is married to another man. It is believed that her husband was away at the time.

"He can't be much of a husband anyway," said *The Scroll*'s palace source. "What kind of husband puts a bathroom on the roof of his house?"

Scandal

This is the first hint of scandal to hit the monarchy since David took over from Saul. His press officer is refusing to confirm or deny the story.

"What the King gets up to on the privacy of his own rooftop is up to him. It's none of our business. And, before you ask, he took the binoculars up because he is a keen bird-spotter."

ADULTERY SENSATION

GENERAL KILLED IN HEROIC BATTLE

Uriah Dies In City Siege

Strange rumours about mystery attack

Uriah the Hittite was reported missing yesterday after fierce fighting outside the city of Rabbah.

Joab (42), Commander of the Israelite forces, reported the loss to the King yesterday.

The King issued a statement yesterday indicating his stoicism in the face of this terrible loss. "The sword devours one man as well as another. We intend to press forward against this city and destroy it. I'm very upset. No, really I am."

Mystery

Military sources, however, remained baffled as to why the attack pressed so close to the walls of the city.

"We had no need to get that close," said one soldier. "We all thought there had been special orders or something. Not only

that, but we were under instructions to attack right where the enemy defenders are strongest. It was suicide."

Rumours persist that the orders came from "on high".

"We believe instructions came from the very highest source," said one officer. "Well, not the *very* highest – I mean that's God. But the next bit down."

Discipline

Uriah was renowned for his iron discipline. Sources report that even on leave his rigorous self-discipline had remained intact. He refused to sleep with his wife or enjoy rich food.

"The King kept encouraging him to go to his wife," said one guest who was at the recent meeting between the two in Jerusalem.

"He kept on and on about it. I thought at one point David was

going to have to draw him a diagram.

"Of course, like any soldier he had a drink or two," reported his butler. "But despite that he just lay down on the mat by the door and slept it off. What can I say? The man was a trooper. He will be sorely missed."

Uriah's widow, Bathsheba, was unavailable for comment.

THE SCROLL Presents...

The Write-Your-Own Psalm Challenge

Response to our challenge has been phenomenal!

Inspired by King David – whose latest collection, *Psalms You Have Loved*, is flying off the shelves of Israel's top scroll-shops – our readers have come up with their own, wonderful devotional poetry.

Here are just some of the entries!

God made the butterfly,
God made the bee,
He really is my favourite
Deity.
Obadiah Bonkers

Pain! The deep madness of despair!
Wire biting deep, blood gashes red!
Maimed and bleeding.
Life ebbs away.
Still, you've got to laugh haven't you?
Mrs Doris Ben Reuben

There was a young man called Nahum
Who thought to himself "this is rum"
Whenever I stand
And march through the land
I get this great pain in my...
Soul, at the sense of my own guilt.
A soldier
(edited by his priest)

I love my little teddy bear
I love my mummy too,
I love the little fluffy lambs
And cows that go "moo, moo".
I love my pretty dresses,
I love my party frocks,
But most of all I love to see
The heads of Philistine warriors, smashed against the rocks.
Rebekah (5)

The Lord is my baker, I shall not want.
He leadeth me by great ovens,
He giveth me currant buns and doughnuts,
My cream horn he filleth to overflowing.
Yea, though I walk through the valley of the shadow of diet
I shall fear no evil.
For thy rock bun and thy Swiss roll comfort me,
Surely goodness and mercy will follow me all the days of my life.
Not to mention abnormally high cholesterol levels.
Dan The Baker
Dan's Kosher Bun House, Jerusalem

God made the butterfly,
God made the bee
He made this lovely padded cell
Especially for me.
Obadiah Bonkers (Again)

FIRST HIS WIFE, THEN HIS LIFE

David In Assassin Love Pact

King David deliberately placed Uriah the Hittite at the front of his troops, so that he could claim Bathsheba – the dead man's widow.

That's the astonishing claim of Nathan the Prophet. What is more, the King had to disguise his actions because Bathsheba was pregnant!

According to a palace insider, Nathan (80) has confronted the King with these allegations, and David has admitted his guilt.

"The King has always had a keen sense of injustice," said Nathan. "When I confronted him with the truth there was no attempt on his part to deny or to hide. He is only too aware of the crime he has committed."

Crime

The truth about David's crime was slow to come out. Suspicions were first raised when, immediately after her period of mourning, Uriah's widow married the King.

"We wondered what was going on," said a neighbour. "And when she gave birth to a son, there was a lot of gossip about whose the child was."

The baby has subsequently died. According to Nathan, this is a direct consequence of the King's sin.

"For every sin there is always a consequence," said the prophet. "No matter how secret the crime, the consequences always

cont. page 76

ADULTERY SENSATION

cont. from page 75

work themselves out for everyone to see."

Extent

Nathan believes that the full consequences of this crime have yet to be seen. According to the prophet, David's own family has been affected by this sin.

"Because of his sin, misfortune will come to the King – from within his own family. For David, nothing can ever be the same again."

One night of passion has had serious consequences for the King. *"Because of this, his family will never be free from the sword," said Nathan.*

Officials Fear For The King's Health
David Fasts For Life Of His Child

David is reputed to have refused all food, slept on sackcloth and prayed desperately for the life of the baby. When the child was pronounced dead, officials feared what the news would do to the King's state of mind.

"We really thought he would lose it completely," said one source. "He was so desperate for this child to live. We were scared how he would react when he was told of its death."

The King realized what had happened, when he noticed some of his officers whispering among themselves.

"He asked us directly whether the boy was dead," reported one officer. "I think he knew what the answer would be."

Recovery

In spite of official concern, the King took the news very calmly.

"He knew that nothing could bring the child back," said one observer. "While the child was alive he was desperate. Now he is resigned to it. I think for him, the child was some kind of symbol."

THE SCROLL SAYS

It is not our policy to revel in the details of the King's tragic personal life.

Instead our aim is to cover these events in a restrained and dignified manner.

But we believe **YOU** – the public – have a right to know.

That's why we are releasing a 48-page, fully illustrated magazine.

David – The Adultery, Rape and Incest Years will be published next week, with a 10-page pull out supplement on *Ten Great Slappers of Israel*.

As ever – dignity is our keyword.

A DEATH IN THE FAMILY

Royal Line In Rape, Incest And Murder

Absalom, son of King David, has killed his brother Amnon in a feud over their sister!

This latest scandal to hit the embattled house of David reveals a tawdry tale of rape, incest and murder.

The story has its origins two years ago, when Amnon (23) raped Tamar (18), his half-sister, having been obsessed with her for months.

"He couldn't stop thinking about her," said his close friend Jonadab. "So, he pretended to be ill and asked if she would come and cook some cakes for him. When she did he grabbed her and forced her into bed. He never even touched her battenburg."

Denial

Jonadab denied having hatched the plan in the first place. "I never meant for this to happen. I was nowhere near at the time. I'm only little. Stop picking on me," he said.

"And anyway, after this Amnon went very weird. His love seemed to turn to hatred and he would have nothing to do with his half-sister."

Mourning

Tamar put dust on her head and tore her magnificent designer dress. "It was a really expensive one as well," said a friend. "She got it from Harvey Nicodemus.

"It was like she was in mourning. She went to her brother Absalom and told him about it. From that moment, he was bent on revenge."

Although King David apparently knew of the rape, he did nothing about it. Officials are denying that this was because of favouritism, Amnon being his first-born son.

Banquet

However, the tale reached its climax when Absalom invited Amnon to a sumptuous banquet during sheep-shearing time. During the banquet, Amnon was brutally murdered by Absalom and his followers, who then fled.

Rissoles

"It was obviously a case of revenge," said Jonadab. "I don't even think Amnon had even got as far as pudding. He was stabbed right in the middle of his rissoles. What a horrible way to go."

Others were less sympathetic.

"He may not have got his pudding," said one, "but he sure got his just desserts."

Disaster

The King has indicated that no action will be taken.

"He seems unable to criticize his children," said one royal watcher.

"If you ask me he's heading for disaster."

IT'S WAR, MY SON!

"King Absalom" As David's Son Declares War

"What a Surprise," Says Unshocked Public

In a carefully co-ordinated coup, Absalom has declared himself King and issued a challenge to his father.

From his base at Hebron, Absalom gave instructions for trumpets to sound throughout Israel as a signal that he has taken over.

"This was about as surprising as a not very surprising thing that usually occurs at a regular time each day," said one royal-watcher. "Absalom has never forgiven his father for his inactivity over all that rape and incest business. And what is more, the boy doesn't half fancy himself."

Absalom is known throughout Israel for his film-star looks and especially his long hair which has inspired a whole new style. Sales of the Absalom look-alike wigs have been enormous.

"*He's gorgeous,*" said one young fan. "*And, unlike his father, he's not afraid to take action. I'm all for it.*"

David, however, has proved suprisingly active. He left Jerusalem with his army in order to regroup his forces.

"The one thing David has learnt is never fight the enemy on their choice of ground," said a source. "I think you may find that the old dog has some new tricks left in him."

Stone Me!

Madman Chucks Stones At The King

As if things weren't bad enough already for the King, he was pelted with stones by a nutter.

The attacker – a man called Shimei – followed David for miles, yelling curses and throwing stones and dust.

"Apparently Shimei is still upset over Saul," explained a soldier. "Some people have long memories. I mean that was years ago."

Mercy

Although several of David's men offered to silence Shimei in the usual way (by cutting his head off) it was the King himself who proved merciful.

"The King took the view that compared to his son being in open revolt against him, a nutter throwing dust was nothing to get worried about."

"*If I were Shimei, I'd be careful. David might be down, but he's not out yet.*"

ABSALOM HANGS OUT

King's Forces Destroy the Rebels

Absalom In Bizarre Tree Death

Absalom has died in a battle which saw a massive victory for the King's forces.

But the young pretender did not die on the field. Instead he was killed because he got his head stuck in a tree!

The forces of the King had defeated Absalom's rebels in the Forest of Ephraim. Although details are still sketchy it is estimated that over 20,000 troops lost their lives.

"Fighting in the forest was awful," said one survivor. "We've lost more men to the forest than to the sword."

Absalom

But the forest claimed its most notorious victim when Absalom was caught in a tree as he tried to escape.

"He was fleeing from some of David's guards when the mule he was riding passed under the branches of a great oak tree," said one witness. "Absalom's head was caught in the branches and he was left hanging there. We didn't know what to do. He was a sitting duck, but no one wanted to kill the King's son."

One Hundred And Eighty

It was commander-in-chief Joab who dispatched the rebel Prince, throwing three metal-tipped darts into the body hanging in the tree.

"I don't think I will ever be able to play darts again," said a soldier.

The dead prince was thrown into a pit and a memorial cairn raised over his body.

King Weeps For Son

Despite the good news of his victory, David is reported as being distraught at the death of his son.

"He just shuddered," said the Ethiopian slave who was sent to tell the King the news.

"Then he went back to his room and started sobbing and wailing. It was as if he'd rather be dead instead of his son."

It was left to Joab again to pull the King together. The Commander-in-Chief insisted that David attend the review of his troops.

"These people had fought for him," explained an onlooker. "The Commander made it clear that if he didn't show them his gratitude then he would forfeit their loyalty. I tell you, that Joab is one tough cookie."

A NATION MOURNS
David Dies, Aged 70

Solomon Is New King
Another Rebel Son Dies

King David is dead. The ex-shepherd who ruled over Israel for forty years has died in his palace in Jerusalem. He was 70.

He had been declining for some time and his last years have been blighted by family dissension, civil war, murder, intrigue among his own army commanders and even a plague which killed 70,000 people.

Nevertheless, he holds a special place in the heart of his people.

"He's the best King we've ever had," sobbed a distraught member of the public. "But then again we've only had two so I suppose that's not saying much."

From early dawn the crowds have been gathering outside the palace in Jerusalem. It is reported that similar crowds are gathering outside David's other homes.

The harpist Eli Jonah has released a tribute single, a version of his famous psalm *Camel with the Wind*.

"I wanted to do something to show my feelings," said Eli. "Also it will be the B-side of my new single." *(Full lyrics on page 81)*

Last Days Blighted By Further Intrigue

Even during the last few months, David's family have been torn apart by plots over who would succeed him.

While the King lay dying, Israel has been a hotbed of rebellion and intrigue. At first, David's eldest surviving son, Adonijah, claimed the throne.

But following David's own wishes, and after securing the support of the King's officers, Solomon was anointed King.

Although Solomon initially granted clemency towards Adonijah, the rebel's political manoeuvring continued.

He tried to marry one of the late King's concubines – a marriage which would give him a legal claim to the throne. The manoeuvre failed and Adonijah has since been executed.

Camel with the Wind

That Tribute Song In Full

Goodbye Israel's King,
Though I never knew you at all,
You had the guts to fight your-
  self,
While others fought for Saul.
Goodbye Israel's King,
From the young man in the
  fifty-second hut,
Who saw you fight Goliath
And sling a pebble in his nut.

And it seems to me, you lived
  your life,
Like a camel with the wind,
Not afraid to make a big noise
When the pain set in.
And I would have liked to know
  you,
But I was just a pleb,
Your were once a shepherd,
And now you're totally dead.

Rebellion was tough,
Toughest road, you ever
  walked,
You made Saul look stupid,
And you were never caught.
And then all your sons,
What a dreadful lot to see,
One attacked your daughter,
And the other was killed when
  his head got stuck in a low-
  hanging and rather unexpect-
  ed tree.

And it seems to me, you lived
  your life,
Like a camel with the wind,
Trudging onwards through the
  desert,
With a painful grin.
And I would have liked to meet
  you,
But I never will,
Your camel let go long ago,
Your legend never will.

Words and music © Eli Jonah.

The Scroll Says

The People's Prince

From humble beginnings, David came to embody the spirit of Israel.

Born the eighth son of Jesse, David was a surprising choice to succeed the disgraced Saul as Israel's King. Yet he went on to great deeds – the slaying of Goliath, the defeat of Saul, the capture of Jerusalem and the victory over the Philistines – all these made David a hero to his people.

Yet there was another side to him as well.

The "Bathsheba in the Bath" scandal, and his inability to curb his tempestuous children showed only too well that David had feet of clay. His many marriages led to disastrous relationships within his family – four of his sons died in attempts to gain the throne for themselves. Ironically, his successor is Solomon, born to Bathsheba, the cause of David's great disgrace.

Perhaps that is what he will be remembered for. Not for the victories, but for the flaws. Perhaps that is why the people took him to their hearts. He was heroic and he was a sinner like the rest of us.

The Scroll says, "Rest in peace your majesty!"

Joab KILL-ted At The Altar

Joab has been killed. A supporter of Adonijah, he was executed clinging to the altar.

Joab (55) was a tough and even ruthless commander.

"He didn't know the meaning of the word fear," said an ex-colleague. "Then again there were lots of words he didn't know the meaning of, like 'mercy' and 'stop hitting me please'. Or 'dictionary', come to that."

Although he is best known for the defeat and execution of Absalom the son of David, his life has also been marked by less glorious acts.

He killed Abner the son of Saul, despite the King's promise of safety. And he murdered Amasa, who had been promised permanent command of the army in his place.

In the end he was killed trying to claim the mercy he had never shown to others. He will not be missed.

THE FAMILY OF DAVID

Your Guide To Murder, Intrigue And Treachery

Here they are, 5 of David's best known sons (excluding Chileab). And to help you judge the best and worst we've given them our very own star rating.

1 **Amnon**
Mother: Ahinoam
A drunkard and lecher who raped and then deserted his half-sister. Killed by Absalom.
Scroll rating: ★
Morals Rating: -★
Intelligence: ★
Bizarre Death Rating: ★★★

2 **Chileab**
Mother: Abigail
Fate unknown. Also known as Daniel, but popularly known as "who?"
Scroll rating: n/a
Morals Rating: ?
Intelligence: n/k
Bizarre Death Rating: ★★ (He was nibbled to death by a giant tortoise. Not really. We made that up.)

3 **Absalom**
Mother: Maacah
Killed while hanging by his head in an oak tree. Rebelled against the King. His big head proved his undoing, in more ways than one. Brave and proud.
Scroll rating: ★★
Morals Rating: ★★
Intelligence: ★★★
Bizarre Death Rating: ★★★★

4 **Adonijah**
Mother: Haggith
Executed by Solomon while attempting a coup. Clearly couldn't organize a brew-up in a pizzeria, as the saying goes.
Scroll rating: ★
Morals Rating: (Didn't know the meaning of the word.)
Intelligence: -★★★
Bizarre Death Rating: ★

5 **Solomon**
Mother: Bathsheba
Crowned King. Second son of David by Bathsheba (the first died in infancy). Noted for his wisdom and sure handling. Has declared an intention to rebuild the temple, something his father never achieved.
Scroll rating: ★★★ Morals Rating: ★★★★
Intelligence: ★★★★★★ Bizarre Death Rating: Let's hope not.

Starting next week: Play Happy Families with *The Scroll*

Join in Happy Families – our super, scroll-tastic competition! Simply scratch off five panels from the scratchcard included with next week's *Scroll* (extra cards available on request). If you've got five different sons of King David, you've won! Careful though – if you find Absalom you'll lose everything!

Happy Families™ is run in association with the King David Memorial Trust Fund.

LET'S SPLIT BABY!

Solomon Solves Riddle Of Baby's Parents By Threatening To Halve It

EXCLUSIVE

A bizarre baby dispute has been solved by Solomon.

Two prostitutes brought a new-born baby before the King in an argument over who was really the mother. One claimed a dead baby had been substituted for her own.

Solomon's decision was that the living child should be cut in half, with half given to each woman.

Begged

"I immediately begged Solomon not to do it," said the real mother. "I asked him to let the other woman have the baby."

Once Solomon heard this he knew who the real mother was since no true mother would submit to having her child split in two.

Critical

Child care experts have denounced the King's conduct.

"I can't believe he did this," said Dr Miriam Stoppit, author of *Child Bisection: The Hidden Dangers*.

"It could encourage parents to treat halving their child as a solution to any domestic difficulties. Admittedly they'd have to be really, really stupid to do this, but as we all know, top-grade stupidity is not a barrier to parenthood."

Wisdom

The judgement has reinforced Solomon's reputation as the wisest ruler in the world.

"He is really wise," said a spokesman. "There is an audible hum from his brain."

The King is an acknowledged expert on plants and animals and every day receives embassies from other countries to listen to his wisdom. He is also an acknowledged songwriter with over 1,000 songs to his credit.

"So far we've been visited by the Assyrians, Amalekites, Phoenecians, Mesopotamians, Egyptians and the Welsh," continued the spokesman. "Although admittedly the Welsh were just lost."

SOLOMON TO BUILD TEMPLE

SCROLL EXCLUSIVE

"It Will Be The Greatest Building In The World"

King Solomon has revealed the plans for the new Temple in Jerusalem.

The building will be a fitting celebration of Israel's God and all he has done for the nation.

"Only the best materials will be used," said the chief designer, Hiram of Tyre (32). "We've got cedar from Lebanon, bronze castings from Jordan, gold from Arabia, and the Welsh have sent some coal. We're not sure what it's used for, but we appreciate the thought."

Seven Years

The Temple will take seven years to build and will use forced labour from all the lands which the Israelites have subdued. The finished building will measure 90 feet long, 30 feet wide and 45 feet high.

"This will be Solomon's crowning glory, I think this temple will be one of the greatest buildings in the world," said his foreman, Adoram.

"It will rank right up there with the Great Pyramid and the Enormous Toilet of Eglon. We have a lot of work to do, but we are determined to bring it in on schedule."

Alternatives

Others, however, have criticized the Temple's design.

"We would have liked to see something more modern," said Perez Bar Mandel, whose consortium had an alternative proposal. "I mean the place is oblong – that's so passé.

"We have suggested a huge dome, with maybe a big figure of Solomon that people could have walked through.

"I think what people are looking for is more than a place to worship God. They want the complete Temple Experience. They want a great day out."

Problems

Perez's ideas have not found popular support.

"There are two main problems," said Hiram. "One, no one's invented the dome yet, and two, he's obviously barking mad."

HERE SHEBA COMES!
Queen Visits King Solomon

The Queen of Sheba commenced her state visit yesterday with a tour through the royal palaces after which she attended a sacrifice in the newly completed Temple.

"The Queen was most impressed with her visit," said her press officer. "She was breathless with wonder at the offerings in the temple, although that could have been asthma."

The Queen (28) is known to have talked for hours with Solomon, testing him with all kinds of difficult questions.

"They discussed many difficult problems," confirmed her officials, "including 'What is the meaning of life?', 'What does occasional furniture do the rest of the time?', 'If all the world's a stage, where do the audience sit?' and 'Who or what are the Welsh?' "

Gifts

The Queen has promised many gifts for Solomon including gold, precious stones and an unknown timber called Almug wood. "As long as it's not more flipping cedar," said one aide.

She will also be sending huge cargoes of precious spices, including cinnamon, mace, coriander and something called the "Madras Extra Hot Stomach Churner."

SOLOMON THE ARCHITECT

Visiting Jerusalem? Don't miss out on these other great attractions.

Royal Palace

Thirteen years in the making featuring the following attractions:

House of the Forest of Lebanon

Like wood? You'll love this house, featuring over 150 feet of cedar wood panels.

House of Justice

Panelled in cedar from floor to beams, visit the scene of the famous judgement. Bring your own baby and threaten to cut it in half, right where the action took place.

Solomon's Living Quarters and the House of Pharaoh's Daughter

A symphony in cedar, built on foundations of the finest stone. See how the King of Israel lives and visit the home of his latest wife. As featured in *Shalom!* magazine.

The Great Court

This impressive stone-floored square is lined with – yes you've guessed it – cedar wood.

So don't miss out. Visit Jerusalem and see the sights.

This article sponsored by Cedar of Lebanon Inc. Traders in fine red wood.

Today's Proverbs

Inspired by King Solomon's wisdom, you've been sending in your proverbs.

Here are some nuggets of gold from YOUR hidden depths of wisdom.

"He who ignores the light gets run over."

Mr G.J., Tekoa

"Good upholstery wins friends, but the way of the wooden bench is hard."

Mrs H.E., Jericho

"A nagging wife is ~~like a dripping tap~~ a very useful sub-editor."

Mr P.I., Damascus

"Many scribes are a blessing, For a King on the throne requires much paper."

Mr B.H., Hebron

"Do not look for the ice house in summer, In winter, leave the tanning oil at home. For nothing goes on forever Except horse jumping."

Maj. Gen. O.B., Tyre

"A wise son listens to his father, But the foolish child forms his own band."

Mrs E.B., Gath

"Never change a nappy during an earthquake."

Mr P. B-J., Gaza

"You would dine with a dribbler? Take a large napkin."

Mrs D., Jerusalem

"The bigger the ears, the bigger the earwax."

Mr P., Ur

"Be angry at the churn and there will be spillage, But true patience produces cream."

Mrs H.K., Kish

"Like water in a dry land, Is a river in a desert."

Mrs H.P., Damascus

"There is a time for everything, Except, perhaps, morris dancing."

Mr J.H., Tekoa

"Like a sinking ship is man, Like a ship that goes down to the depths of the sea, For we all have holes in our bottoms."

Mr. A.H., Nazareth

"All come from dust and to dust we all return. So, be careful with that hoover, for you sweep up my ancestors."

Mrs H.H., Samaria

"The world is like an onion, The more you peel it, the more you cry. Also it's round. And you can have it in salads."

B.J., Jerusalem

"Consider the elephant, Mightiest of beasts, Slow and sure, But oh! The nosebleeds! For nothing is without suffering."

Head Keeper, P., The Zoo, Rabbah

"A bird in the hand is a bit messy."

Rev. C., Jerusalem

Send your proverbs to our proverb editor,

Agur, Son of Jaheh

2nd Wisest Person in the World

3, no tell a lie, 4 Temple Courtyard, Jerusalem.

DOING THE SPLITS

Reheboam In The South, Jeroboam In The North

Following the death of his father Solomon, Reheboam has taken charge of the Kingdom of Judah. But the rebel Jeroboam has gained control of the rest of Israel.

There seems little hope of avoiding a partition now, with the Northern Kingdoms ending up in control of a man who rebelled against Solomon.

Solomon's declining years were a shadow of his early reign.

Foreign Gods

"This crisis has been a long time coming," said one political commentator, putting the blame down to Solomon's increasing interest in foreign gods.

"He started worshipping Astarte, the Sidonian goddess, Milcom, the famous abomination of Ammon and The Queen of Sheba's Exotic Spice Girls," said one priest.

"He should have known that God would be angry. It was only for his father's sake that he let Solomon alone as long as he did."

Wives

Others pointed to his physical decline.

"I mean, the guy had seven hundred wives and three hundred concubines," said his doctor. "That kind of thing takes its toll. He must have been worn out with the shopping, never mind anything else.

"For the world's wisest man, he didn't half do some stupid things."

NO BAAL GAMES ALLOWED

SCROLL EXCLUSIVE

Elijah Beats The Prophets Of Baal In Mount Carmel Showdown

It was billed as the title decider – a contest to prove who was the real God of Israel.

On one side, the prophets of Baal; four hundred and fifty prophets specially picked by Queen Jezebel. On the other side, Elijah, a hairy, old bloke.

The challenge facing them each was to call down fire from heaven, to ignite a bull on a sacrificial bonfire. The deity who answered their call was to be declared the winner.

Hopping

The Baal boys started first. From morning to midday, they danced round the bull, in their strange hopping dance.

continued on page 89

"Their God didn't answer them," explained Elijah (67) later. "I asked if he was on the bog or something, but they didn't answer. They just went on and on and on.

"It's as I've always said, you'll never win anything with the long Baal game."

Water

Elijah's turn came later. And just to make things more difficult he had the fire drenched three times in water.

"I wouldn't want anyone to think I was cheating," he explained.

He stepped forward and prayed to God. Immediately, fire rained from heaven and the bull was roasted.

Delight

The crowd went wild with delight, burst through the crash barriers, ran onto the pitch and immediately slaughtered the false prophets of Baal.

"Technically it's an offence to run onto the pitch," said a steward, "but seeing as how these people are bloodthirsty maniacs, I think I'll just slip away quietly."

A grim, but satisfied, Elijah looked around him at the people celebrating the return of Israel to following God.

The contest also foretold the ending of the drought which has afflicted the land for years – a drought many attribute to the nation's idol-worship.

"They think the drought's over," Elijah said. Then, spotting a small cloud in the sky, he added,

"It is now."

IT COULD BE JEHU

Time runs out for Ahab after Elijah meets God in a cave

In a tersely worded press release, Elijah has indicated that Jehu will be anointed the next King of Israel.

"I have encountered God in a cave," said Elijah, "which is a nice change from the usual kind of creatures that lurk in these places. There was a hurricane, then an earthquake, then a fire. Then a still small voice. That was the Lord. And he told me, time's up for Ahab."

Unrepentant

Ahab remained unrepentant, however, having already threatened Elijah with death if he shows his face again.

"The wife and I are fed up with the old codger," said the King. "I mean, it's getting so that you can't worship false gods in an orgy of depravity without him telling you off. After all, we're young. We're only having fun."

"He's so old fashioned," agreed Queen Jezebel. "This is a multi-faith society now. If people want to worship Baal, visit temple prostitutes and sacrifice their children, I think we should respect that.

"This is a society built on free speech. And anyone who disagrees will be executed."

Elijah Appoints Successor

Elijah has appointed Elisha as his successor. The lad – a teenager from the Horeb region – was a surprise choice.

"He's not got the experience," said a fellow prophet of Elisha. "And he needs to change his name. It sounds like someone sneezing."

THAT'S VINE!

Ahab Steals Vineyard For Royal Allotment

Naboth Framed In Royal Stoning Plot

Ahab has stolen a vineyard, just so he can have an allotment next to his palace. What is more, he's had the owner framed and stoned to death.

The owner, Naboth, was falsely accused of cursing God and the King. He was immediately taken out and stoned to death. Ahab quickly took possession of the vineyard he had long coveted.

The plot was revealed by Elijah, who has told the King that he and his wife will die and his blood will be licked up by dogs.

"I always said the monarchy was going to the dogs," said one eyewitness, "but I didn't mean it literally."

Ahab, though dismissing the curse, is taking no chances in his preparations for battle against Ramoth in Gilead.

"I'll be leaving the Chihuahua at home," he confirmed.

Burn Rubber Baby

Elijah Taken To Heaven In Fiery Chariot

Elijah has been taken to heaven. But he didn't die – he was transported on a FIERY chariot.

The event was witnessed by his apprentice Elisha, who now claims to be TWICE the man his predecessor was.

Double Portion

"Elijah asked me what I wanted, and I asked for a double portion of whatever it was that he had. At first he thought I meant his chips, but then he realized I was talking about his power.

"He didn't know if that could be granted, but he said if I saw him leaving then I would know my request was granted."

Chariot

Before Elisha could reply Elijah was carried away.

"This fiery chariot and horses appeared from nowhere and he was lifted into heaven," explained Elisha.

"Either God has taken him, or he has just been run over by a jumbo jet."

ELISHA GRINS AND BEARS IT

"Slaphead" Jibe Results In Bear Attack

THE SCROLL SAYS

Is this the greatest prophet ever?

Elisha has been breaking the world prophet records throughout Israel. Here are just a few of his miracles:

● He miraculously created oil for a hard-up widow to sell, saving her from bankruptcy
● He brought back a boy from the dead
● He removed the poison from a big vat of tomato soup
● He miraculously multiplied loaves so that there was enough for everyone
● He made a metal axe head float
● He set huge great grizzly bears on irritating brats
● Tax Inspectors smile at him.
It's an impressive CV. Perhaps one day someone might come along who can do better.
But that person would have to be God himself.

Elisha (28), the prematurely balding successor to Elijah, revealed a new weapon in disciplining children: setting the bears on them.

The children gathered around Elisha on the road to Bethel.

"They were making fun of him, shouting 'slaphead' and 'hurry up baldy' and stuff like that," said one parent. "He turned and cursed them."

The next minute two bears appeared from the forest and set on the children. Forty-two were savaged.

"Speaking as a teacher," said the boys' headmaster, "I am appalled at this act. Speaking as a human being, however, I have to say that there were a large crowd of us cheering on the bears."

HOW THE MIGHTY ARE FALLEN

Queen Mother Jezebel Thrown From Window

Ahab's Sons Killed In Battle

The Queen Mother is dead.

Jezebel (83, or 53 in dim light) was executed yesterday at the command of Jehu, the new King.

"She was always an evil, spiteful woman," said one solider. "As Jehu arrived, she leaned out and more or less told him he wouldn't last.

"I think she was expecting a battle of wits, but he just had her thrown out of the window. Now, that's what I call a witty riposte."

After that the new King went and ate and gave instructions for the body to be recovered. But when the servants went to get it, all they could find was her skull, feet and hands.

"The dogs had eaten the rest," said a servant. "There was nothing left to bury.

"To be honest, she was always a bit of a dog's dinner."

Victory

Jehu (40) defeated Ahab's son at the field of Naboth – the very field Ahab stole.

"You could see that Jehu was fired up for the battle," said a soldier. "He drove there like a madman. I've never seen a chariot move so fast. It was a really bad case of chariot rage."

The new King tore into the enemy forces. Joram, King of Judah, tried to run away and was hit in the back with an arrow.

Purge

Jehu will now concentrate on purging the country of all the Baal worship introduced by the late Queen.

"If I were a prophet of Baal I would think seriously about taking a long holiday," said an official.

"When this guy takes a dislike to you, he doesn't muck about."

SCROLL MOTORS — A Look At The Latest Chariots

HARD DRIVE
Jehu's Chariot – One Mean Machine

By Jeremiah, Son of Clark

This is one mean baby.

No gold on this chariot. No leather trim. No in-chariot stereo – leave the trumpeter at home.

Jehu's chariot is about one thing and one thing only: going very fast indeed.

Fast

If this chariot were an animal, it would be a cheetah.

If it were a curry it would be an extra-hot vindaloo with added chillies.

If it were an elephant it would be a great big grey thing with flappy ears.

If it were a gerbil it would be very difficult to stand on.

If it were any faster, it would be illegal. In fact it *is* illegal, but when you're the new King, you change the laws to suit.

Engine

The engine is a twin-horsepower, 84 litre pair of stallions, offering 8-hoof drive and emitting a deep, throaty roar (especially if they've had a lot of clover to eat). If you want the turbo-charged option they give you another horse and a bigger whip.

Tyres

The reins feel taut and responsive. The tyres are big – built to eat up those suspension-hungry desert roads.

As an add-on, you can have large, sharp blades built into the wheels, allowing you to cut through that rush-hour battlefield with ease.

Speed

But it's the speed which startles you. From the first flick of the whip, the chariot surges forward leaving the rest of the traffic behind, along with the contents of your stomach.

It zooms from 0–60 in less time than it takes to say, "Please don't kill me." Which explains why Jehu never lets anyone off. He simply can't hear them.

Face the facts: this chariot is as fast as a very fast thing that's fallen off a cliff. If it were to go any faster, you'd meet it coming back.

And you can't say faster than that.

Jeremiah is a presenter on Top Chariot.

NEXT WEEK: The Jordan Jericho – a new MPV with "extra crumple zones".

Chariot Racing Results
Damascus Grand Prix

1. Dagon Hilkiah
   (River Jordan)
2. Micah Hakkatan
   (Williams-Reuben)
3. Micaiah Shunammite
   (Locust)

WHAT'S ON...

Your Guide to the Best TV

8.00 GOOD MORNING ISRAEL
With Reuben and Jael

The early morning programme that really brings the day alive.

Today we will be looking at fashion with advice on how to get the right veil to fit you. Levitical Hygiene expert will be advising on women's problems and how to achieve ritual purification. There will be advice on new and exciting colour schemes for your tent, while Jane from the tribe of Asher will be creating a cake in the shape of the Holy of Holies.

10.00 THE MORNING SACRIFICE

This morning's service comes from The Temple in Jerusalem where the High Priest will slaughter a sacrificial bullock. Followed by coffee and discussion.

12.55 THE WEATHER PROPHECY

What the weather will be like at some point in the future. Possibly at the end of time, depending on the range of the prophet involved.

1.00 THE NEWS

Followed by **LOCAL NEWS** from your tribe.

1.30 KINSMEN

Another episode of this exciting new soap about a group of families, living together in tents in the same tribe. Today Uzziah is caught playing with his father's urim and thummim. Will Rebekah keep her mouth shut, or will he be taken outside the camp and stoned to death?

2.00 PSALM FOR THE DAY

Another uplifting Psalm from the pen of Ethan the Ezrahite.

3.00 BLUE PEREZ

Children's Magazine. This week the presenters will show you how to make a scale model of Mount Ararat out of some old lolly sticks and a bit of sticky-back sackcloth.

3.30 GRANDSTAND

Live coverage of the camel racing from Jericho. Followed by the derby match between Amalekite Athletic and Moabite United.

6.00 THE BOOK OF THE LAW
See Highlights

7.00 THE ANTIQUES TRAIL SHOW

Coming this week from Jerusalem. Discoveries include a sword reputed to have belonged to Goliath, a Baal-worshipper's sacred pole, and two gate posts from Gaza, which could be the ones that Samson nicked.

9.00 A PARTY POLITICAL BROADCAST ON BEHALF OF KING JOSIAH

Since this is a one-party country this might be a bit pointless, but the King is keen to keep you informed.

9.30 MEN BEHAVING RIGHTEOUSLY

Another hilarious episode in the life of two Levites sharing a flat. This week Nahum finds an unusual use for an ephod of grain, while Tobit has problems keeping his phylacteries on!

10.00 QUESTION TIME

From the Central Courtyard, Jerusalem. Panellists include the prophet Isaiah (who will bang on about the threat of Babylon again), the priest Hilkiah and the King's minister Asaiah.

Highlights
THE BOOK OF THE LAW
Part Six: Clean and Unclean Animals
Following the recent discovery of the Book of the Law during repairs to the Temple, Hebrew TV is continuing its coverage of the public reading. King Josiah will continue to read out the commandments and decrees with subtitles for the hard of hearing and expert analysis from a rabbi and a top voice-over artist.

PROPHET HOOKS UP WITH A HOOKER

Hosea Is Living Metaphor

Hosea the prophet has married a well known prostitute.

In what must count as one of the world's more unlikely marriages, the prophet of God has married a girl known locally as "Lino Lil".

What's more, he claims GOD told him to do it.

"I think the whole thing is some kind of metaphor," Hosea (35) explained. "I know what this girl is like. She'll be unfaithful to me at the first opportunity. In fact, I happen to know she got off with the best man at the reception. And the head waiter, the organist and the photographer. And I couldn't help noticing that the officiating Priest had a strange smile on his face."

Unfaithfulness

It is thought that Hosea's actions are intended to illustrate God's love for Israel and Israel's relentless unfaithfulness.

"God is obviously making a point," said one observer. "I mean, her heart's in the right place. Unfortunately it's the rest of her that is never where it's supposed to be."

"Strange as it seems," said Hosea. "I really love her. Despite the fact she's a complete slapper. No one is beyond love."

EZEKIEL SEES DANCING BONES

"Performance Prophet" Sees Into The Future

The prophet Ezekiel has returned from an unnamed valley where he claims to have seen bones dancing.

"There were bones everywhere," said the prophet. "It was like the Old Folk's Club at Mamre. Only these were dead, instead of just not moving."

Then, according to the prophet, the bones started to join together.

"All these bones, the remnants of some mighty battle, were knitted back together by God. They were given flesh and muscle and breath.

"God told me that Israel is dead, but it will come alive again."

Ezekiel (42) is well known for his "flamboyant" prophecies.

"We must not forget that this is the bloke who lay on his left side for 390 days just to point out Israel's guilt," said a spokesman for the Semitic Prophet's Union (SPU).

Performance

"This is the man who baked his bread on cow dung. This is the man who cut his hair off, weighed it, and burnt some of it, while throwing away some of the rest. He is a performance prophet.

"*Whether he's accurate only time will tell. At least he's entertaining.*"

"Exile"

Much of Ezekiel's prophecies have to do with an impending "exile". He believes that Israel will be packed up and carted away by a foreign power. This even extended to him miming the disaster, climbing through a hole in the wall with his suitcase.

Experts were unimpressed.

"Whatever impending doom is hanging over Israel," said one, "it can't be as bad as watching his mimes. He'll be doing that thing where he pretends to be trapped in a box next."

Ezekiel was unrepentant.

"I have seen the winged creatures with wheels on," he replied, unhelpfully.

HI HO, HI HO, TO BABYLON WE GO!

Israel Taken Into Captivity

Temple Burnt And City Walls Demolished

SCROLL EXCLUSIVE

Centuries of neglect and disobedience have resulted in the complete defeat of Israel and Judah.

Now the entire population is to be taken into captivity by Nebuchadnezzar, Emperor of Babylon.

"We have no one to blame but ourselves," said the prophet Jeremiah (72). *"For three hundred years, since the age of Solomon, it has been a succession of evil kings and queens."*

In Babylon, the Israelites are expected to act as slaves.

"It's Egypt all over again," said one Israelite. "I'm not looking forward to going to Babylon. I hear they hang gardeners there."

Unpopular

Jeremiah, who has been arrested, tried and thrown down a sewer because of his messages, says that captivity has been coming for years.

"They wouldn't listen to me. They wouldn't change their ways. I told King Jehoiakim, I told King Zedekiah. There was nothing they could do."

Blinded

The final siege of Jerusalem took six months. The King was captured and has since been blinded and deported to Babylon in chains. Understandably he is reported to be depressed.

"If you've just been blinded, it's hard to look on the bright side," said one Israelite.

The Temple of Solomon has been burnt to the ground. "The smell of burning cedar wood was almost suffocating," said a witness.

Some Israelites have fled to Egypt.

"It won't do them any good," said Jeremiah. "They will all be killed."

Depressed

When asked if all this didn't make him depressed, Jeremiah replied, *"It's being so cheerful as keeps me going."*

Surprisingly, he says that Israel will return.

"Jerusalem will be re-established,' he said. "A descendant of David will sit on the throne of Israel. God will save us.

"Only not yet."

PHEW, NOT A SCORCHER!

Fiery Threesome Are Too Hot To Handle

Three government officials who refused to obey the law found an amazing loophole today, when they WALKED through fire!

Their fiery fate was supposed to punish them for their refusal to worship the King. But the fire made no difference to them – they just sang and danced around!

"I've never seen anything like it," said an astonished palace guard. "We built the fire up specially, but these guys just wandered around like they were out for a stroll! Then they began to sing!"

Miracle

The three government workers – Shadrach (25), Meshach (27) and Abednego (24) – are all local officials in the Babylonian County Council. They are giving the credit for their miraculous escape to their God, who they claimed walked around in the fire with them.

The fire is thought to have been one of the hottest on record – so hot in fact that several workers were burnt to death as they threw the victims in. Union officials are even thought to be threatening action for possible breaches of health and safety regulations.

"Never mind the people in the furnace," said a shop-steward, "several of my men got very nasty sunburn."

U-turn

Following this remarkable occurrence there are rumours of a government u-turn with a relaxation of the previously strict local idol worship laws. A spokesman for King Nebuchadnezzar described the King as "gobsmacked".

Dream Reader Gets Top Post

Babylon's new Governor got the job by interpreting the King's dreams.

Daniel was appointed to the post after correctly interpreting one of the King's many visions. A spokesman for the personnel department said, "This appointment flies in the face of our equal opportunities policy."

Guess

Government officials, however, are insisting the test was a lot tougher than just interpretation.

"Daniel had to guess what the dream was in the first place," they insisted. "That's like getting the right answer to the question, when you don't even know what question's been asked."

IS THE KING A LOONY?

Has Nebuchadnezzar lost the plot?

That's the question being asked in government circles following the latest bizarre events.

Consider the evidence. In the past few months he has:

- MADE a giant golden statue of himself
- DREAMED all kinds of weird dreams
- ORDERED everyone to worship him
- STARTED to listen to bagpipe music

What next? At this rate it won't be long before he starts eating grass and going "moo".

The Scroll *says "Pull Yourselves Together Your Majesty!"*

Have Your Say

Is the King nuts? Or just lovably eccentric? Join our phone poll.

Dial 01 for "I think the King is one pot plant short of a hanging garden"

Dial 02 for "I think he's doing a great job and please don't throw me to the lions!"

THAT'LL COME IN HANDY

Divine Graffitti Reveals Bleak Future For New Emperor

"Tickle Our Parsnips!" Advises Ghostly Handwriting

Daniel Called To Interpret

A mysterious message appeared on the wall of the imperial dining room, while the King was giving a feast!

Belshazzar (34) was hosting the annual "Isn't the King great" banquet, provided by noblemen who wish to stay in his good books, when a hand appeared and began to write on the wall.

"We were gobsmacked," said a waiter who happened to be standing nearby. "This hand appeared out of nowhere, and started writing near the lampstand. I mean it's bad enough a ghost appearing, without them starting to vandalize the place."

Even more mysterious was the writing itself, which was both illegible and indecipherable.

"Most of us thought it was some kind of prescription," explained an official. "But we brought a chemist and even he couldn't explain it."

Daniel

In the end, Daniel (30), the famous soothsayer, was summoned.

"He was promised great rewards if he got the answer right, but he didn't seem very interested in that," said an onlooker. "He just said 'many, many, tickle your parsnips. I think it might be a reference to the King's love life."

Weighed Out

In fact the message was *mene mene tekel parsin*. Daniel pulled no punches in his interpretation.

"The King has been weighed in the balance and found wanting," he said. "His kingdom will be divided between the Medes and the Persians."

Belshazzar, although impressed, refused to cancel the feast.

"He's very clever," he said of Daniel, "But I don't think anything's going to happen really."

When The Writing Was On The Wall...
Belshazzar Found Murdered
Darius Takes Over

In a lightning coup, Darius the Mede invaded after yesterday's banquet.

Hard information is hard to come by in the chaos that is occupied Babylon. There are rumours that Belshazzar has been killed by the invaders.

"I thought a mede was a small lake," said one observer. "Still, I suppose being invaded by a broad expanse of water will be good for the hanging gardens."

"Darius is 62 years old and will govern the kingdom with three administrators," said an informed source.

An uninformed source said, "I haven't got a clue what you're on about."

Daniel Still Dreaming

Daniel has had another dream, according to close friends.

"He dreamt of four beasts coming out of the sea," said a colleague. "The first was a lion with wings of an eagle, the second was a bear. The third was a winged leopard with four heads and the fourth had ten horns and teeth of iron."

The Scroll asked leading dream analysts to interpret these dreams.

"I think the meaning is clear," said Dr Baz Shazbazzaz of the Babylonian Nocturnal Studies Institute. "He has a morbid fear of becoming an estate agent. It's perfectly normal."

Daniel did not agree. "This is the future," he said. "These are four empires. And in the fourth one, a great hero is going to come along, someone sent by God."

No timetable for the empires has been given, although the first is thought to be Babylon, and the second the Medes.

"The fourth may be a little known country called Rome, although you can never rule out the Belgians," said an expert.

OUR LIONS ARE VEGE-TARIAN

Daniel Survives The Lion's Den

Daniel, the disgraced dream-reader and ex-governor, is back in favour again, after an astonishing tale of survival.

He had been sentenced to death following tough new religious laws brought in by Darius the Mede. Darius declared that everyone should pray to him. Anyone disobeying this rule was to be turned into Kit-e-Kat.

When Daniel (40) refused to toe the line, the King had no option but to throw him in.

"Darius wasn't happy about it," said an official. "But he'd signed the law. And, according to the laws of the Medes and Persians, these decisions are irrevocable, even when manifestly wrong. It's a bit like soccer referees."

"Daniel's enemies had manoeuvred the King into this position. They'd planned it all."

Lions

But, although Daniel was thrown into the pit, he emerged completely unscathed. The King rushed along the next day and discovered, to his joy, that Daniel was still alive.

"I can't understand it," said their Keeper. "Those lions should be ravenous. They've only had a pot of yoghurt each in the last week."

Daniel was lifted from the pit and, in his place, those who accused him were thrown into the lion's den.

Before they'd even hit the floor, the lions jumped on them and tore them limb from limb.

"That's a relief," said the Keeper. *"For a moment there I was worried they were ill."*

The Scroll
Behind the Big Frilly Fern Thing
Seventh Ziggurat
Hanging Gardens of Babylon

PLEASE RELEASE ME, LET ME GO

Jerusalem To Be Rebuilt

Nehemiah Given Lottery Money

Nehemiah, the cup-bearer to King Artaxerxes, is to lead an expedition to rebuild Jerusalem.

And what is more he has been given substantial aid from the King to help him with the project.

"I received news about the state of the city from a relative," said Nehemiah (42). The card which was sent by his cousin Hanani simply read, "Weather awful, few who remain dying of dysentery, walls in ruin, gates burnt. Glad you're not here."

"Immediately I decided to ask the King to release me."

Supplies

The King agreed to the plan and has provided supplies from royal funds including timber from the royal forests. "As long as it's not more of that flamin' cedar wood," said one builder.

"I am aware that there will be people around whose interests will be threatened by the rebuilding," said Nehemiah. *"But I am determined to push it through. The walls will be rebuilt. The city will be repopulated. We are coming home."*

Local Councils Opposed to Building Scheme

The scheme has met opposition from local leaders.

"It will cause too much traffic," said Sanballat the Horonite. "I mean, all those lorries with building materials travelling to and fro. We'd like to see a Damascus bypass built first."

Ezra, who has already been in the city for some time, was scathing in his criticism.

"These people want to see Jerusalem remain in ruins. They will even attack us if they can. Well, let them try it.

"You can do some horrible things to people with a trowel."

CYRUS SPELLS FREEDOM!

Cyrus Releases The Babylonian Captives

Jews Will Return Home

Cyrus, whose Persian army swept through Babylon only days ago, has released the Jews from captivity and allowed them to go home.

The people from Judah and Israel have been exiled in Babylon for seventy years. Now they will be going home. They will be taking with them much of the loot taken from the Temple in Jerusalem by Nebuchadnezzar's troops.

"Nehemiah has already built the walls," said one source. "Now we can finish the job. We want to rebuild the temple, the houses and even the old public convenience on the corner of Shalom Street. We have waited a long time for our freedom. It is time we had a place of our own again."

Dedication

The Israelites will be led by Ezra and the prophet Haggai.

"There is much to learn," Ezra said. "I am sure if we re-dedicate ourselves to the law of God we will be stronger than before. I want to build a country so strong that we will never be conquered by another nation again."

"You'll be lucky," said another traveller.

The Scroll

A Makeshift Hovel
Just Behind the Dung Gate
Jerusalem

Bluff Your Way Through History

As Jerusalem is rebuilt, we present a *Scroll* Guide to all those memorable Kings of Judah and Israel. (And many you'd prefer to forget.)

Saul
(Unified Israel)
Frankly, a boo-boo. Still, we all make mistakes from time to time.

David
(Unified Israel)
Great King, great psalms, big problems.

Solomon
(Unified Israel)
As wise as a very wise old owl with a lot of A-levels. Went downhill when he discovered women.

Jereboam 1
(Israel)
Split with Judah. The cold war begins. Evil-doer, idol worshipper, the daddy of all the bad eggs who followed.

Rehoboam
(Judah)
Strong-arm negotiator, rebel. He worshipped foreign gods and even allowed sacred male prostitutes. Succeeded by his son...

Abijah
(Judah)
Who was just as bad as his Dad.

Asa
(Judah)
A good King. Followed God and tore his grandmother off a strip for making a "repulsive sacred pole." The mind boggles.

Nadab
(Israel)
Meanwhile back in Israel. Idol worshipper. Only ruled two years. Murdered by...

Baasha
(Israel)
As bad as the bloke he butchered.

Elah
(Israel)
Became King on the death of his father, Baasha. Got out of his head at a party and was struck down by the Captain of his chariots, a bloke called...

Zimri
(Israel)
Killed Elah and murdered the rest of his family. Ruled for seven days before commiting suicide by setting fire to the royal palace. Did this because he was about to be deposed by the Army commander whose name was...

Omri
(Israel)
Little is known of this King, which is just as well, as he was worse than anyone else before him. Which is saying a lot. Founded Samaria and was then succeeded by his son, the supreme stinker...

Ahab
(Israel)
Married Jezebel, worshipped Baal, nicked vineyards, framed innocent men, annoyed Elijah, the list is endless. Killed by an arrow which sneaked between the joints of his armour. His blood leaked into the bottom of the chariot and the dogs licked it out after his death. Serves him right.

Jehoshaphat
(Judah)
Followed his father Asa as a generally good egg. (His grandmother stayed right away from lewd poles.)

Ahaziah
(Israel)
Baal worshipper, son of Ahab and chip off the old block. Fell out of a second-storey window in his palace in Samaria.

Jehoram
(Israel & Judah)
Took over both countries for a brief spell, but as bad as the rest of them. Killed by Jehu the boy-racer.

Ahaziah
(Judah)
Ruled Judah for one year until he was fatally wounded by...

Jehu
(Israel)
He drove the fastest chariot in the west. Massacred the prophets of Baal. Not exactly perfect, due mainly to his habit of killing anything he didn't like, but a big improvement on previous monarchs.

Athaliah
(Judah)
The only Queen in this list, but hardly a member of the gentler sex. She was about as gentle as Goliath on a bad day. Mother of Ahaziah, she became Queen by murdering anyone else who might have had the remotest claim. The only ones who survived were the palace cat and the baby Joash, who was spirited away by a nurse and hidden. She reigned for six years before the priest Jehoida organized a coup. According to the histories, she was "killed in the horses' entry" which sounds extremely nasty.

Joash of Judah (Judah)

Only seven when he came to the throne, he created new tax structures, restored the worship of God and still had time to play with his action man. Ruled for forty years, until he was assassinated at the hands of his servants. Perhaps he didn't tip them enough.

Jehoahaz (Israel)

Another rotter.

Amaziah (Judah)

A good king, who let a victory over Edom go to his head. He challenged Judah and lost heavily.

Joash of Israel (Israel)

And another baddie...

Jereboam II (Israel)

Politically strong, militarily successful, but his kingdom was falling apart. The poor got poorer, the rich got richer and he was still worshipping foreign gods.

Uzziah (Judah)

A good king. He came to the throne at 16 and reigned for fifty-two years. Unfortunately, for most of that time he was confined to his room with the worst case of acne ever recorded by man.

Zechariah (Israel)

Another scumbag. Murdered by...

Shallum (Israel)

Who ruled for one month before being done in by...

Menahem (Israel)

Who reigned for ten years and was attacked by the Assyrians.

Jotham (Judah)

Son of Uzziah, good bloke ... and, er, there you have it really.

Pekahiah (Israel)

Reigned for two years before he was assassinated by his equerry, who was called...

Pekah (Israel)

Who in turn was assassinated by...

Hoshea (Israel)

The last King of Israel. The Kingdom was destroyed by the Assyrians and Hoshea deported in chains.

Ahaz (Judah)

Just when you thought it couldn't get any worse. He sacrificed his own son, and couldn't pass a fancy tree without offering to some disgusting foreign god.

Hezekiah (Judah)

One of Judah's finest kings. An invasion by the Assyrians was thwarted when 185,000 troops were struck down by God with the plague. Unfortunately he was followed by...

Manasseh (Judah)

Judah's version of Ahab. Enough said, really.

Amon (Judah)

Killed by his own house servants. Just as bad as his Dad.

Josiah (Israel)

A good King, who discovered the book of the law in the course of repairing the Temple. Josiah insisted on a programme of public readings, to remind the people of what they had been missing.

He died at Megiddo, killed by Pharaoh Necho. A sign of things to come.

Jehoahaz (Israel)

Only reigned for three months, before he was deported by Pharaoh, who put him in chains. Died in Egypt. Pharaoh installed...

Jehoiakim (Israel)

Renamed by Pharaoh, ruled for eleven years before the Babylonians invaded. After that the writing was on the wall.

Jehoiachin (Israel)

Taken into exile in Babylon, along with his mother, 7,000 top men, 1,000 blacksmiths and the palace cat.

Zedekiah (Israel)

A puppet King who rebelled. Nebuchadnezzar had him blinded and taken in chains to Babylon.

So there we go. Forty-three Kings, most of whom you really wouldn't want to meet in a dark alley, and some of whom you wouldn't want to meet in a well-lit alley with nice wallpaper.

As Israel is restored and Jerusalem is rebuilt there is a sense of optimism, of hope. There is a looking forward to good rulers, and to a new way of leading.

Looking back at this lot, you have to say, "Don't hold your breath."

HAVING A WHALE OF A TIME!

Jonah Invents The Submarine

SCROLL EXCLUSIVE

Jonah the prophet arrived in Nineveh yesterday, after three days and nights in the belly of a FISH!

The prophet had been called by God to go to Nineveh, but had fled in the OPPOSITE direction.

"I boarded a ship bound for Tarshish," explained the waterlogged prophet. "I just wanted to get as far away as possible."

But, no sooner had the ship hit the open sea, than a hurricane blew up.

"We drew lots to find out who was to blame for the storm," said Jonah (36). "*Personally, I tried to put it down to El Nino, but it was soon discovered that my disobedience was the cause. I volunteered to be thrown into the sea.*"

Fish

Even then, that wasn't the end for Jonah. Instead he was swallowed by a huge FISH that happened to be passing.

"I think, technically speaking, it was an enormous aquatic mammal, but let's not quibble," said Jonah. "All I know is it smelt of herring. I wouldn't recommend spending a long weekend in a whale's stomach. It was worse than Skegness."

Vomited

Eventually, the fish deposited Jonah on the beach.

"I don't want to go into the details of how I got out. Let's just say I was hurled onto dry land."

Jonah proceeded to Nineveh to preach God's message.

"If they don't repent then in 40 days they will be destroyed," he said.

The response to his message is reported to be favourable, leaving Jonah depressed.

"*If they're just going to repent, I might as well have stayed at home.*"

SCROLL SPORTS

All the Action All the Time

Racing from Canaan
The 3.30 Prophet's Handicap

> The big race of the day, featuring a fine field of well-known prophets. Here are the runners and riders, with a guide to form.

Isaiah
The "grand old man" of the field. Married, with two sons, this prophet is popular with the literary punters, having several books to his credit, including a History of the Reign of King Uzziah, and his own book of prophecy. The favourite, and rightly so; although slight fluctuations in form have led to accusations by some scholars that he is actually three different people.

Amos
How life has changed for this shepherd from Tekoa! A good starter, but finds it difficult to keep on when the going is hard. Themes of social justice and inequality always make for challenging racing.

Joel
The son of Pelhud comes from Jerusalem and is strong on repentance. Much of his previous form has been in prophesying huge plagues of locusts. So, any dark, fast-moving clouds over the course and Joel could be your man!

Obadiah
The book is very short on this runner (about 21 lines). Strong on punishment of Edom, but form suggests long distances are beyond him.

Micah
This peasant from the town of Moresheth is certainly not a thoroughbred, but is always popular with the punters, on account of how he spends most of his time attacking the rich and the leaders of Israel.

Nahum
Out of the small stables at Elkosh comes this little-known runner, who, up till now, has concentrated on prophesying the fall of Assyria and the destruction of Nineveh. Perhaps too much of a specialist.

Habbakuk
Little is known of this runner besides the fact that he, like Nahum, is very much an Assyrian-destruction specialist. And his name sounds like a load of chickens. However, he is not lacking in confidence, given that several times in his work he questions God and raises significant issues. One to watch.

Zephaniah
A real thoroughbred. The product of the royal stables, his bloodline goes back to his great-grandfather King Hezekiah. A strong runner, with a good all-round message. His call for the rejection of false gods might prove to be a loser with the general public, most of whom like to hedge their bets when it comes to religion.

Haggai
What can I say? His name is the plural of Haggis. A bit of a "dark horse", this one, concentrating on the restoration of Israel.

Zechariah

The priestly entry. Zechariah is based at Jerusalem having returned from Babylon, where he proved a successful and versatile runner. Strong on rebuilding the temple.

Eric

Not in the Bible at all.

Malachi

The youngest in our field, but proving very popular with the public due to his strong criticism of priests.

Ezekiel

What can you say about this brilliant, but eccentric prophet? Trained in the Exile Stables, Babylon. His visions border on the psychedelic and his habit of acting out God's prophecies have made him a real crowd pleaser. Specializing in prophecies of the fall of Jerusalem, he could romp away from the rest of the field, or he could just as easily stop and pretend to be a tree. Has suffered much for his sport.

Jeremiah

Another of the grand old men of the field, this fiery, powerful prophet is at his best when the going is heavy and the distances are long. His strength and endurance are legendary, as is his supreme grumpiness. Prophecies of disaster and doom to Judah have led to several rich owners throwing him down holes.

Hosea

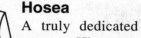

A truly dedicated runner, His marriage to Gomer the Prostitute remains one of the most powerful metaphors in the Bible. Hosea is understandably strong on Israel's unfaithfulness to God, but could tire easily due to chasing his wife around town all day.

Has three children called "God Scatters", "Not Loved", and "Not my people." They are responding well to counselling.

Yesterday's Results

JERICHO

Going: Rough
1.00: 1 BAAL BAAL BLACK SHEEP Levi Piggott (5–1); 2 Ehud's Chariot (4–7 fav.); 3 Tickle My Parsnips (10–1). 5 ran.
1.30: 1 BALAAM'S ASS Phileas Dettori (100–1); 2 Roadside Angel (2–1 fav.); 3 What's That Horse Doing on the Course? (A mistake). Only 2 supposed to run.
2.00: 1 RED URIM Reuben Champion (3–1); 2 Mind My Scrolls! (33–1); 3 Moses Supposes (5–1). 8 ran.

RED SEA

Going: Soggy
2.00: 1 THE BELLY OF THE PILCHARD Jonah Francome (1000–4 and a bit); 2 Reed Basket (10–1); 3 Ark The 'Erald (30–1). Pharaoh's Army was a faller.
3.30: 1 AARON YOUR HEAD Gideon Richards (30–1); 2 In a Manna of Speaking (2–1 fav.); 3 Moses' Plague-ground (Quarter to six). 650,000 wandered.

SODOM and GOMORRAH

Going: Salty
4.30: THAT'S YOUR LOT Perez Scudamore (3–1000); 2 Unnatural Vices (Evens fav.) 3 Brimstone and Hail (Uneven surface). Thousands ran.

TEENAGER IN LOVE
Carpenter Denies "Rumours"

A Nazareth-based carpenter is to marry his teenage bride, despite the fact that she is pregnant.

The village is abuzz with rumours and innuendo. According to the girl herself, the whole thing is a miracle.

"This angel appeared to me," said the girl, who as a junior cannot be named for legal reasons*, "and told me I was going to have a baby. Naturally I was confused. I mean, I don't know a lot about the process, but I know a man has to be involved somewhere. But the angel insisted that the baby will be the son of God."

Convinced

Joseph (48), her husband-to-be, was ready to call off the marriage. Now it appears that even he has been convinced.

"God visited me in a dream and told me what was going on," he said to our reporter. "Now get out of my shop before I hit you with this mallet."

The Nazareth Child Support Agency has praised Joseph's choice. "I think we'd have had quite a lot of trouble calculating the amount of maintenance the father should pay otherwise," they said. "I mean, what is a reasonable figure for the owner of the world?"

Sceptics

Most of her neighbours in the village are sceptical of the girl's claims.

"I can hardly believe that God would choose her," said one woman. "This is obviously just an attempt to jump the housing queue. You wait, when the baby comes it'll be the red-carpet treatment. Private hospital bed, all mod cons. And it'll be the tax-payer who foots the bill. They only do it for the benefits."

Although her name rhymes with "hairy".

Keeping It In The Family

Elizabeth, the cousin of the teenager at the centre of the "divine pregnancy" row, is also pregnant, it was revealed yesterday.

Although getting on in years, she and her husband Zechariah are expecting their first child.

"It's a miracle," she said. "Well, two miracles really, because not only am I pregnant, but God has struck my husband dumb as well. I can't believe that two of my dearest prayers have been answered at once."

According to Zechariah, he was struck dumb after being visited by an angel, while on duty in the temple.

Temple leaders are sceptical, however. "This is the house of God," said one. "We have rules and regulations here. No angel would be allowed in, unless all the right forms had been filled in."

UTTER NON-CENSUS

Caesar Augustus Announces Census

Citizens Have To Register At Birthplace

In a huge administrative feat, Caesar has ordered a census to be taken of the entire Roman empire.

"Being a tyrannical occupying power takes a lot of management," said Quirinius, Governor of Syria (44). "We want to know how many people we can order about."

Services

When asked what point this census would serve, the Governor said, "It will help us plan for the provision of public services, such as aqueducts, roads, public floggings, etc.

"*Most importantly, however, it will mean a lot of pointless inconvenience for our subject people. Which is really what being an occupying power is all about.*"

Money

"There are only two reasons for holding a census," said an expert. "Either to register people for military service, or to check up on tax-paying.

"*Since Jews are not eligible for the army, one assumes they simply want more money out of us.*"

Pointless

All family members have been told to report to their place of birth in order to register.

"This is a thoroughly pointless exercise," said one opponent of the scheme.

"*All the Romans want to do is make us bomb around the country filling in forms. This is an utterly senseless census.*"

The Census Form Revealed!

In an exclusive scoop, *The Scroll* has managed to obtain a copy of the census form which subjects of the Roman Empire will have to fill in.

Roman Digest
Governor's Office, Jerusalem

Dear **Mr Joseph**

It's your lucky day! Our computer has chosen you to be included in our ROMAN DIGEST prize draw. What's more – you are already a winner! That's right! Everyone who receives this letter has already won a handy travel alarm* worth 5 sestertii!

All you have to do is go to your home town and fill in the form. You will then be able to claim your free gift and will be entered in the lucky Roman Digest Draw.

OFFICIAL CENSUS FORM

Write on one side of the paper and don't forget to fill in your name and address.

Name:..

Tribe:..

Age 14–17 ☐
18–25 ☐
26–35 ☐
36–50 ☐
Very Old Indeed ☐
Dead ☐

Occupation
Farmer ☐ Innkeeper ☐
Peasant ☐ Rat-Catcher ☐
Prophet ☐ Soldier ☐
Carpenter ☐ Revolutionary ☐
Pharisee ☐ Messiah ☐
Chariot-Mender ☐
Other.......................... *(Please specify)*

What do you think of the Roman Empire?
Excellent ☐ OK, for a dictatorship ☐
Poor ☐ Up the revolution ☐

How could we improve our services?
More aqueducts ☐ Less floggings ☐
Better drainage ☐ More theatres ☐

Any idea who the present Emperor is?
Tiberius ☐ Nero ☐
That Bald Bloke ☐ Claudius ☐
Caligula ☐ A Horse ☐
Another nutter.................................
(Please be specific)

Where would you like us to invade next?
Brittania ☐ Ethiopia ☐
Hispania ☐ Hibernia ☐
Diptheria ☐ Hernia ☐
Hypothermia ☐ Ruislip ☐

Tie-breaker – Complete in 25 words or less
I love being ruled by the Romans because...
....

☐ Occasionally we may make your name known to other invading nations offering a similar product. Please tick the box if you do not wish to receive any promotional material.

*Actually a parrot with insomnia

A STABLE RELATIONSHIP

Baby Born In Cowshed

Housing Shortage Blamed

THE SCROLL
Just below the star and to the left, Bethlehem, Judæa

A baby has been born in a cowshed, because there was no room in the hotels.

The mother, a teenage girl, was travelling with her husband to register for the census.

"There simply wasn't anywhere else to put them," explained the manager of the hotel. When asked whether he hadn't been unnecessarily greedy, he replied, "What do you mean? I've given them a ten per cent discount haven't I?"

Health Scandal

The case highlights the appalling state of Bethlehem's public health services. Despite it's position as a provincial centre, it doesn't even have a hospital.

"That's because they haven't been invented yet," explained a local government official. "The other reason is that no one really cares about the poor anyway. Especially not poor people who get themselves pregnant."

While Shepherds Watched

Shepherds Serenaded By Holy Choir

A group of Bethlehem shepherds have reported how they were serenaded by a heavenly choir of angels.

"The angels were celebrating the birth of a child," they explained. "We were told to go down into the village and see who we would find."

"I've never seen anything like it," said one shepherd. "The sky was full of these beings. I knew they weren't like us. For a start they were clean."

Their employer was sceptical of their claims.

"I think they've been drinking the sheep dip," he said. "It can get very cold on those hills. You get to imagining all kinds of things."

Aliens

Others, however, are claiming the shepherds have been visited by aliens from another planet.

"For a start there's been this strange star in the sky," said one UFO expert. "Secondly, it's not unusual for alien beings to visit earth and sing to you. I myself was witness to a spectacular concert some years ago, when aliens appeared to me and sang excerpts from the Psalms. Admittedly I haven't seen so many since I've started taking the tablets, but that doesn't prove anything."

WISE MEN LOOK FOR A STAR

Scientists Visit Herod

Wise men from the East have visited the King in a search for a new-born Prince.

"They seemed to think that this star we've been seeing is some sort of portent," explained the King's press officer. "Naturally, Herod was most interested, given the fact that he is the reigning monarch. He has asked to be kept in touch with events."

The foreign delegation have headed towards Bethlehem. "We are very grateful for all the King's advice," said one of their delegation, when asked what they thought of the King.

"We will try to keep him fully informed of anything we discover."

Another of their party was less tactful, *"If he thinks we're going to tell him where the boy is he must be stupid as well as barking mad."*

Gifts

The wise men have even gone to the extent of buying gifts for the new King – frankincense, myrrh and gold.

"Peculiar gifts, if you ask me," said one observer. "Gold is always welcome, but surely it would be better to set up an off-shore trust if you want long-term investment?

"Frankincense, however, is a sacrificial incense and myrrh is for perfuming dead bodies.

"Maybe I'm old fashioned, but I would have thought that a nice doll or some bootees might have been more suitable than joss sticks and embalming fluid."

SLAUGHTER OF THE INNOCENTS

Herod Does An Uncanny Impression of Pharaoh

In a macabre echo of centuries past, Herod (67) has ordered the death of hundreds of young boys.

The boys, all hailing from the Bethlehem area, have been slaughtered as a result of the King's increasing paranoia.

"After the wise men left, Herod grew increasingly anxious," said an aide.

"They had promised to contact him – he had even given them a supply of mobile carrier pigeons in order to send messages back. When they failed to report back the location of the supposed 'prince' he ordered drastic action."

The King ordered the death of all boys under two years old.

"No one is going to take my throne," he said. "I'm sorry, but I'm not taking any chances." Herod has long been ranked among the class-A nut-ters of the ruling elite, but even this has left political commentators agog.

Shocked

People in Bethlehem were understandably shocked at this turn of events.

"He's a madman," said one. "He's insane. All the children have been taken. It's a dreadful day in our history.

Escaped

Some, however, made it out before the slaughter.

"The only people who escaped were those who got lucky," said a Bethlehem resident.

"I know of one couple, for example, who left for Egypt with their baby boy only a few days ago. The guy had had some dreams or something. Anyway, they upped and left on a battered old A-reg donkey.

"Maybe they knew what was going to happen."

SNAKES ALIVE!

John Condemns Crowds As "Vipers"

John the Baptist (33), the itinerant preacher, has accused his listeners of being "vipers".

"They must turn and repent," he said. "They must be baptized. The axe is coming – any tree which fails to produce good fruit will be for it."

Jordan Safety Warning

John has been baptizing people in the river Jordan – an activity which has been condemned by health and safety inspectors.

"Have you seen that river?" they asked. "No wonder he asks people to make their peace with God before he dunks them. There's a very real chance they won't survive the experience. You might as well empty a toilet on someone's head."

Since emerging from the desert a few weeks ago, John has created a considerable stir in the media.

"I just love his style," said one teenage fan. "I mean, look at the dude's clothes – camel-hair tunic and a leather belt. It's so simple. Not many people could carry that off. Mind you I think being wild-eyed and slightly fanatical helps."

Trouble and Strife!

John Criticizes Herod's Marriage

John has criticized Herod's recent marriage to Herodias.

The Tetrarch has married the ex-wife of his brother, which would be OK, except for the fact that his brother is still alive.

"This is the modern world," said Herod. "John has to accept that relationships change.

"For many despotic, slightly mad monarchs, keeping their marriage together is an impossible strain."

Immoral

"This marriage is immoral," thundered John. "Not only is Herodias his brother's ex-wife, she is also Herod's niece.

"In anybody's book, we are talking about a dysfunctional family."

Split

When Herod the Great (the famous baby butcher) died, he split the Kingdom between his four sons – a decision that has caused some argument. Now Herod has persuaded Herodias to leave his brother Herod Philip and marry him.

"Call me old fashioned," said John, "but I don't think stealing your brother's wife is a move guaranteed to calm family relationships."

LOCUST GRATIN PLEASE

Restaurants And Fashion Houses Jump On The John Bandwagon

Jerusalem's fashionable restaurants and haute-couture houses are jumping onto the John the Baptist style wagon with their new offerings.

At top restaurant *Le Manoir Aux Forthcoming Apocalypse*, the head chef has devised a new menu based around John's diet.

"We're offering a confit of honey and truffles for starters, followed by stuffed locusts on a bed of river weed for the main dish." When challenged about the high prices they were charging he replied, "It's very labour intensive. Have you ever tried to stuff a locust? No one can do it easily. Except, perhaps, another locust."

Fashion

Meanwhile fashion houses, too, are jumping on what the media is calling "Repentance Chic".

"Camel hair is the new fabric," said design guru Jeff Banksofthejordan. "It's so versatile. Not to mention brown. And smelly."

High-street manufacturers the *House of Levi* have created special camel-hair jeans, while top fashion house *Red Sea or Dead Sea* have brought out coats, tunics and even underpants.

"The underpants are a very challenging statement," said their PR agency. *"They really focus the mind on this repentance issue. For a start you're sorry you ever put them on."*

John Baptizes Cousin

During one of his mass baptisms yesterday John baptized his own cousin.

"John seemed strangely reluctant," said one onlooker. "Normally you can't stop him from dunking people, but this time it was as if he wasn't up to it."

Others reported hearing voices after the event and even seeing a bird settle on the man's head.

"Something weird was happening, but after a fortnight eating locusts I could have been seeing things."

MOVE OVER JOHNNIE THERE'S A NEW KID IN TOWN

Jesus The Healer Draws Huge Crowds

Following the recent media furore over John the Baptist, there is another new contender – Jesus of Nazareth.

The preacher and teacher is causing a stir throughout the region, with large crowds flocking to hear him from Jerusalem, Judæa and even Syria.

"He's certainly the hot ticket," said a well-known tout. "He can heal, he can preach, he can cast out demons, he can make the blind see, and he even turns water into wine. This lad can do it all."

Every day, tales of his miraculous powers are heard. Lame people are walking, blind men are given their sight.

Recruits

Jesus (33) has even started recruiting a team to organize things for him. In a surprising move, his recruits include four fishermen and a tax-collector.

"I think this shows how immature he is," said a leading Pharisee. "No one with any shred of decency would have anything to do with a tax-collector. And as for the rest of his rabble, well the best you can say of them is that they smell of fish.

"Rest assured, this is a nine days wonder. He will never amount to anything."

PIE IN THE SKY

SCROLL EXCLUSIVE

Jesus Stands On The Mount And Asks For Miracles

In his first major policy statement, Jesus of Nazareth has emphasized the poor and dispossessed. But his speech also called for a level of behaviour that many people felt was impossible.

"I don't think he's being realistic," said one listener. "There was a lot about 'loving your enemy'. What's the point of that? If you love them they aren't your enemy any more, are they? You'll have to find some new ones – and that takes a lot of hard work."

Poor

Much of Jesus's emphasis was on poverty.

"Blessed are the poor," he began. "For theirs is the Kingdom of Heaven."

The message went down well with his listeners, many of whom were so poor they could hardly pay attention.

But after this promising start, he began to make more and more demands on his listeners.

"He claimed that it was as bad to think of murdering someone, as it was to actually do it," said an irate listener. "I couldn't believe he said that. I could have killed him."

Dentists

And dentists are up in arms over his repudiation of revenge.

"In Exodus it clearly says we are to take eye for eye and tooth for tooth," said one. "Now Jesus comes along and says we shouldn't live that way. It's a disgrace. Us dentists have special rates for revenge work. We stand to lose all that if he has his way."

Others, however, were more complimentary.

"I don't think anyone can deny that this guy really has got hold of something," said one. "You only have to read back issues of *The Scroll* to see what all this revenge stuff leads to. If we can learn to forgive one another, if we can learn not to judge, then maybe we could really change the world."

Jesus Come Home
He's Probably Bonkers, Say Relatives

Jesus's relations have asked for a court order to let them take charge of him. His mother and brothers have gone to Capernaum, where Jesus is currently living.

"We think he's lost his mind," said his seventh cousin, once removed. "I mean, we're a respectable family. We can't have him traipsing all over the country. I think he must have had some kind of accident in his dad's shop. Maybe a hammer fell on his head or something."

THAT'LL COME IN HANDY
Jesus cures on the Sabbath

Pharisees are furious that Jesus has cured a man with a withered hand on the Sabbath!

"It goes against all the laws," their spokesman said. "The Sabbath should be a day of rest. It should not be frittered away 'healing' people. He did this deliberately to annoy us."

"I think he did it as a kind of gesture against the Pharisees," said the man who was healed. "I've never been able to use this hand, but it's as good as new now. And I tested it by giving the Pharisees a gesture of my own."

It's All Too Much!
Rich Man Claims Subscription Is Too High

A rich young prince who asked Jesus how to get eternal life was told to give all his money away, it was revealed today.

"I was gobsmacked," said Prince Reuben Farquhar-Ben-Very-Rich-Bloke (21). "I don't mind putting the odd bob in a collection plate, but everything! That's nearly all I've got!"

Riches

Jesus used the occasion to point out the dangers of being rich.

"I understand what he was saying," said one onlooker, "but speaking as a beggar, I wouldn't mind living dangerously occasionally."

Camel

Jesus went on to claim that it was easier for a camel to go through the eye of a needle, than for a rich man to enter heaven.

"Aha! I think I've called his bluff on that one," said Reuben. "The fact is, that camels *can* go through the eye of a needle. All you have to do is purée them first."

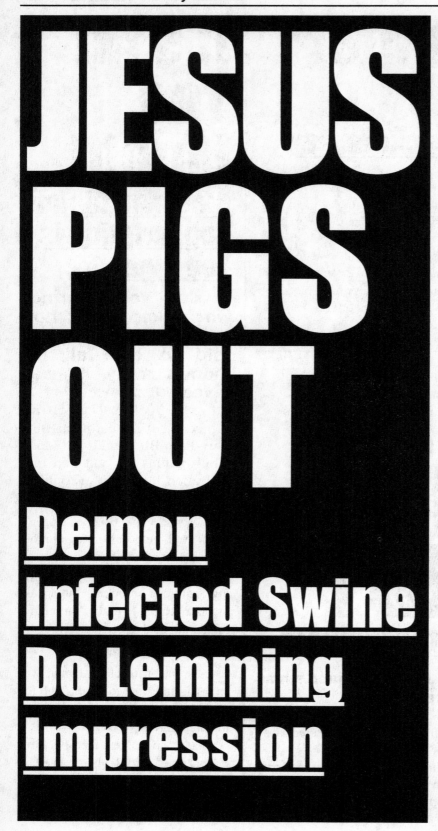

JESUS PIGS OUT

Demon Infected Swine Do Lemming Impression

Jesus of Nazareth cast demons out of two men today, and made the demons go into a herd of pigs. The pigs subsequently threw themselves into the lake and drowned.

"I'm livid," said the owner of the pigs. "One minute they were snuffling about and doing normal piggy things, the next thing, they're completely barking and trying to do the breast-stroke. It was mass porcicide."

Now the owner intends to sue and the people of the town have asked Jesus to leave.

"I had a big order ready to go to make up *Big Abdul's Pig in a Bun Special*," he said. "Very popular with the Roman soldiers they are."

Miracle

"It was obviously a miracle," said the town's mayor. "And granted these two men had been so violent that it was impossible for people to even walk by them.

"*But you have to ask yourself, 'What next?' Rabid chickens? Daffy Ducks? Cows jumping over the moon? We can't afford for this bloke to go around the country-side using our livestock as dust-bins for unwanted demons.*"

Impressed

Even the Mayor, however, had to admit that he was impressed with the miracle.

"Obviously I'm pleased for these two blokes," he said. "And I have to admit it made a great spectacle. I particularly enjoyed the pig that did the triple somersault with a tucked pike. Several people watching gave him a perfect six."

Ding Dong! Kingdom Calling!

Jesus Sends Out Disciples On Doorstepping Mission

Jesus has sent out his twelve closest aides – the so-called "disciples" – on a "meet-the-people" tour.

Working in pairs, the disciples have visited several towns and villages where they have, according to reports, performed miracles and preached what they call "the Kingdom of Heaven".

"They were very nice young men," said Dolores Oldperson (74). "They've cleaned my Reuben up beautiful. He had leprosy, but now it's all gone. I shall certainly be voting for them in the future."

Identity

The disciples have been forbidden by Jesus to carry any money or to take any possessions with them.

"I think they ought at least to have some kind of ID card," said one citizen. "After all, you get all types on your doorstep these days. Only the other day, I had one of those Jehovah's Insurance Salesmen or whatever."

Another citizen said, "They heal the sick, cast out demons, and give blind people their sight back. Who do you think they are – the Gas Board?"

Tax Collectors Call For Code Of Conduct

Too Many Members Repenting

Members of the Tax Collectors Guild have called for a strict code of conduct following the high-profile repentance of some of their members.

"As Tax Collectors, it's important that we don't pursue popularity," said the Guild's chairman, Ezekiel Tax Ben Efit (84%). "We are, at the end of the day, in the extortion business. Not only do we work for the Roman authorities, but our habit of charging more than the official rate has led to us being hated and feared. It would be a pity to lose all that." The call follows in the wake of two high-profile cases where Tax Collectors have given money back.

"No tax collector in any place at any time should give money back," said the chairman. "People like Matthew and Zacchæus have acted in a hot-headed and generally irresponsible manner."

Influenced

Their behaviour is thought to be influenced by the fact that Jesus has had meals with both of them.

"Whenever this Jesus chap eats with people they start acting totally out of character," said the chairman. "If you ask me I think he's putting something in their tea."

HOW TO GET AHEAD IN DANCING

John Loses His Head Over Salome's Dance

Herod Antipas has beheaded John the Baptist as a reward for his step-daughter.

Salome (17) performed her saucy dance at his birthday party, and Herod promised to give her anything she asked. She asked for the HEAD of John the Baptist.

"We were amazed," said one guest. "You don't expect a young woman to ask for someone's head on a plate. I'm sure Herod had in mind some make-up or a pair of tights or something."

The King imprisoned John after the prophet denounced his marriage to Herodias, his brother's former wife.

"Despite the fact that John denounced him, Herod didn't want to have him killed. But there you go – he always was a lecher. That girl knew exactly how to get what she wanted."

Herodias

It is thought that Salome was put up to it by her mother, Herodias, who was furious at John's criticism.

"I'm pretty sure Salome didn't think of it," said one palace source. "She's a complete airhead. I detect her mother's hand in this."

Although John's body has been taken away by his followers, no one knows where the head has ended up.

"Try Herodias's fridge," was one wry comment.

Although Jesus has been told the news, no comment has been forthcoming from him.

"Jesus always praised John," said one source. "In fact he claimed that John was to be the forerunner of the Messiah. He must be upset – after all, John was his cousin. But also there's nothing new in this. This is the way that all the Kings have treated their prophets."

JESUS FEEDS FIVE THOUSAND

"He Cut The Bread Very Thin," Claim Sceptics

In one of his greatest miracles yet, Jesus fed 5,000 people using nothing more than five loaves of bread and two fish.

"This has to go down as one of the greatest catering-based miracles," said an expert. "There were even twelve basketfuls of left-overs."

The miracle took place after a huge crowd had followed Jesus into the wilderness to hear him preach. Jesus had retreated there for privacy, but his reputation meant that hordes still followed him.

"When he saw how far they'd come and how hungry they were he asked people to come forward with provisions. The only volunteer was a young lad and his fish sandwiches. Jesus prayed, broke the bread and gave it out. Somehow it just kept going."

Sceptics

Others, however, were sceptical of the "miracle".

"There must be a simple explanation," said a leading Pharisee. "Maybe he did it with mirrors. Or perhaps he just used very thinly sliced bread. He's obviously invented the smoked salmon sandwich."

Jesus
Miracle Worker, Maniac or Master Chef?
You Decide
Write to *The Scroll*
The Fifth Stall to the Left of the Dove Salesman
The Temple Courtyard
Jerusalem

Weather

It will be a stormy night tonight throughout the region. Readers are advised not to go out in boats on lakes and not to attempt to walk on water.

Tempest-force winds will be experienced in all areas, unless some miracle occurs.

TREES A JOLLY GOOD FELLOW

Jesus Cures Blind Man

A blind man cured by Jesus said that people looked just like walking trees.

The man, from Bethsaida, had been brought to Jesus by friends. When asked if he would cure him, Jesus SPAT in his face.

"I thought, at the time, there was no need for that," said the man. "I mean, all he had to say was 'no'. Then I realized he'd put some on my eyes."

Jesus asked him if he could see anything.

"I could see these dim shapes," said the man. "They looked like trees. Then I realized they WERE trees – I was staring at an olive grove."

Moving Trees

He was turned round to see the people.

"I saw these other shapes like trees, but they were walking."

Now he has his sight back.

"I can see everything very plainly," he said. "Unfortunately, that includes my relatives. Some people should be heard and not seen."

BACK FROM THE GRAVE

Lazarus Walks Out Of His Tomb After Doctors Pronounce Him Extremely Dead

In an event reminiscent of the ancient prophets, a man came back from the dead today.

Lazarus (32), a resident of Bethany near Jerusalem, popped his clogs four days ago. But when Jesus visited the tomb and called to him, he hopped out of the cave.

"He was all wrapped up in embalming rags," said a witness. "He looked like he'd lost a fight with the Andrex puppy."

Death

"I can't remember very much about it," says Lazarus. "I remember lying ill in bed and asking the doctor how bad it was. I knew it was serious when he advised me not to start any big jigsaw puzzles."

When Jesus heard of the death of his friend he insisted Lazarus was only sleeping. But as Jesus got nearer the tomb, he wept.

"I don't know why he was crying," said one. "Maybe the idea of death just got to him."

Stench

At the tomb, Jesus asked for the stone to be rolled away.

"We were all prepared for a stench," said an onlooker. "After all, this is Israel. It's not exactly a deep freeze out there."

But they were even more amazed when Jesus called and Lazarus emerged from the cave.

This is not the first person Jesus has brought back from the dead. Others include a Centurion's daughter and a widow's son.

"They were probably never dead at all," said one sceptic. "It's all just trickery. Any roads, I'd like to see him do the trick on himself."

ADULTERESS LOSES STONES
Woman Rescued From Stoning

A woman caught in the very act of adultery has been rescued from certain death by Jesus.

When the woman was brought before him he simply asked anyone who had never sinned to throw the first stone.

"Naturally we couldn't do that," said one participant. "So we all went home. No one had the heart to stone her after that."

"All the time he was writing on the ground with his finger," said one participant. "He was just doodling. It was so annoying.

"I mean, there's nothing more guaranteed to put a damper on a good old-fashioned execution than someone not paying attention."

Following Jesus' challenge the angry mob drifted away one by one.

"He just looked at this slut and told her to go away and not to do it again. Where's the punishment in that?"

Fun

Jesus's act was condemned by a leading Pharisee.

"He shouldn't go around spoiling people's innocent fun," he said. "This was supposed to be a festive occasion. People had been looking forward to it.

"Some even brought along their favourite stone."

Hero's Welcome
Jesus Enters Jerusalem
Palm Trees Now Seriously Endangered

Jesus entered Jerusalem yesterday to scenes of near riot.

Huge crowds had gathered to witness his entrance. Many of them grabbed palm leaves and started to wave them about. So much so that environmental campaigners have complained about deforestation.

"The whole place was awash with palm leaves," complained one. "Jerusalem used to have lush, green palm trees. Now we've just got a collection of big twigs."

Some even spread their cloaks on the ground to welcome him – a brave move as he was riding a young donkey at the time.

"You know what donkeys do when they're nervous," said one onlooker. "Well, let's just say they won't be wearing those cloaks again in a hurry."

A PAIN IN THE TEMPLE

Jesus Clears Out Money Lenders

Whatever happened to "Blessed are the peacemakers"? Says Shocked Trader

High Level Talks About "Messiah"

In the midst of Jesus's triumphant entry into the capital, it is rumoured that secret discussions are taking place between the chief priests and the city elders.

Rumours that they are discussing how to undermine the popularity of Jesus were denied by spokesmen.

"These were just routine meetings," said one. "Obviously we're not keen on some of his activities, but that doesn't mean we'd actively plot against him, does it?"

Following his triumphant entry into the city, Jesus went straight to the Temple and THREW OUT all the tradesmen!

"He was really steamed up," said a stall-holder. "I don't know about 'gentle Jesus meek and mild', the way he picked up my stall and threw it through the air was positively superhuman."

Jesus was reacting to the trading activities that take place in the outer court of the Temple. Here traders sell doves, sheep and cows for sacrifice and change currency to pay the Temple tax.

Legitimate

"We have a perfectly legitimate trade," said the Chairman of the Temple Board of Commerce. "All we are doing is finding a niche market and filling it. I don't think we deserve to be called robbers and thieves.

"I don't think there's anything wrong with what we do. Many people treasure things like the little model of the Temple that gets covered in Manna when you shake the bottle. And the shirts which say '*My Husband Went To Worship And All I Got Was This Lousy Tunic*' sell like hot cakes."

Support

Jesus's move apparently had popular support.

"People are fed up of being ripped off," said one visitor. "Have you seen the price of those doves? Jesus was striking a blow for all of us. I don't see why worship should cost us so much. It was great watching him chuck all their stuff out the door."

The High Priest was unavailable for comment last night.

JESUS HAS SMELLY FEET

SCROLL EXCLUSIVE

Woman Pours Perfume On Preacher's "Plates"*

While resting at a village called Bethany, Jesus had his feet washed – in perfume!

The gesture was made by a woman fan, who upended her bottle of expensive scent over Jesus's feet while he was eating his meal.

His disciples were reported to be furious.

"Do you know how much that perfume cost?" stormed one. "We could have sold that and given the money to the poor. She could have used peppermint foot lotion. It's very reasonably priced and available from most branches of Sandals."***

Jesus (36) was more laid back about it – hardly surprising since he was reclining at the time.

"He said this was a good work," said one witness. "I think he saw it as sort of symbolic. But then he sees everything as sort of symbolic."

Nard

The perfume – *Caleb Klein's Pure Nard* – is one of the most expensive on the market and comes in the form of a thick ointment. It is thought the woman spread nearly a pound of the stuff on Jesus's feet, before wiping it off with her hair.

"We cannot recommend this type of practice," said a leading Jerusalem hair dresser. "Whilst it might make the hair smell very nice, it is extremely greasy. Frankly, once the smell wears off she'll have stone*** like a chip pan."

---

* "Plates of sacrificial Passover meat" = feet. Pharisee rhyming slang
** Jews don't wear "Boots".
*** "Stone That Harlot Over There" = hair. More Pharisee rhyming slang.

JESUS ARRESTED

"Messiah" Taken
Into Custody

Things Were Getting Out Of Hand, Say Authorities

Jesus has been arrested. The troops grabbed the so-called "Messiah" as he was praying with his disciples among the olive trees.

It is thought the dawn raid was guided by Judas, one of the preacher's former disciples.

"Mr Judas has very bravely put his knowledge at our disposal," said the High Priest. "It proved what we thought all along – this Jesus is an offender against Jewish law, a subversive revolutionary and a danger to the stability of our nation."

In the scuffles one of the High Priest's servants lost an ear. Even while being dragged away, Jesus healed the man.

"I'm very grateful," said the servant. "It would have made it very difficult to wear my glasses."

Trial

His disciples were scattered and Jesus himself taken to the High Priest's house to face a committee of Jewish civil and religious leaders. The few witnesses to the events inside say that the argument was very heated. Those who saw Jesus subsequently say that he looked bruised about the face and was covered in spit.

"We categorically deny he has been beaten," explained a member of the council. "He simply fell off his chair into someone's fist. It happens a lot."

No date for the trial has been set.

PONTIUS PILATE DON'T BE DUMB! JUST SET FREE THE JERUSALEM ONE!

Cut out and wave during demonstrations

"MY HANDS ARE CLEAN"
Pontius Washes His Hands Over Jesus's Fate

Pontius Pilate, the Roman Governor of Judæa, has refused to intervene in the row between Jesus and the Jewish authorities.

Although he could find no grounds for formal complaint against the self-styled "saviour", Pilate (42 or possibly 57, whichever you'd prefer) eventually bowed to pressure and, in a symbolic gesture, washed his hands of the whole affair.

"Pilate said he was innocent of Jesus's blood," said one critic. "Seeing as he then handed him over to his own soldiers to be whipped and crucified, I think he may need to look up the definition of innocent in the dictionary. He appears to think it means 'Here, let me kill him for you.'"

Truth

Pilate's decision – or lack of it – is hardly surprising. In the few years he has been here the Governor has built up a reputation as a man who only gets off the fence to ask other people what they think.

"The only decision he ever makes is not to decide," said a critic. "The man has less spine than your average sea slug. He's not interested in the truth. He wouldn't know the truth if it came up and slapped him."

Barabbas Freed in Passover Deal
Success for *THE SCROLL*'s Campaign
In a related incident, Pilate freed Barabbas, the so-called "Jerusalem One". Another success for *The Scroll*, the powerful paper and the people's voice!

Mystery In Courtyard

Witnesses report a mysterious Galilean lurking near the hearings.

"I thought he was a follower of Jesus, but he denied it," said a servant girl. Another person claimed to have seen the Galilean by Jesus's side.

"I put it to the bloke, but he swore at me and denied all knowledge of Jesus. Then, when a load of others questioned his accent, he started swearing at them and claiming he never met the man."

The encounter finished when the mysterious intruder heard a cock crowing.

"He immediately burst into tears," said a witness. "I don't know why a cockerel should affect him so much. Perhaps he just hates chickens."

IT IS FINISHED

Great Adventure Ends In Death

The man who promised so much is dead. Jesus, the preacher who, only a few days ago, was being hailed by the crowd as the King of Israel was crucified at midday, dying three hours later.

The soldiers made a cruel parody of his claims – crowning him with brambles and dressing him like a King. They even nailed a sign over his head reading "The King of the Jews".

The man, who claimed to be God's son, was taken to a rubbish dump on the edge of the city and killed. Some of the women who had followed his career were there with him, including, it is thought, his mother.

"We can mock, but once again our hopes have been shattered," said an onlooker. "We thought he was the one to save Israel. He couldn't even save himself."

He has been taken to the grave of a wealthy supporter and buried in a private ceremony.

Freak Earthquake Hits Jerusalem

Temple Curtain Goes For A Burton

Jerusalem was shaking yesterday as a freak earthquake and unusual atmospheric conditions plunged the city into darkness.

"The ground shook and rocks split in half," said the Chief Weather Prophet. "There were even reports of tombstones rolling away. It was a serious earth tremor."

Curtain

The ground shook so much that the huge curtain in the Temple was split in half. The curtain guards the most sacred place – the Holy of Holies – from ordinary, unholy people.

"I heard this enormous tearing sound," said one worshipper. "For a moment I thought my trousers had gone, but then I saw this curtain was ripped from top to bottom. There was chaos. The Priests were trying to stick the curtains back up before anyone could get a look. Luckily somebody rushed in shouting, 'let me through, I'm an interior decorator!' and the situation was saved."

Darkness

Along with the earthquake, Jerusalem was plunged into darkness for three hours.

"Clearly the earthquake cut the power supplies," said an official. When it was pointed out to him that we didn't actually have any power supplies, he said "Oh."

When asked what was causing these severe conditions, the Chief Weather Prophet said, "It's probably just an area of high pressure. In the old days they would have attributed this to the wrath of God. Thank heavens we're all a bit more sophisticated nowadays."

YOU SEEN ANYBODY ROUND HERE?

Jesus's Body Missing From Tomb

Two women who went to anoint Jesus's body have reported that the body is missing from the tomb. What is more, they claim to have met him!

The tomb was protected by two armed guards, not to mention a huge stone rolled in front of the doorway. The women claim that an angel removed the stone and then sat on it.

"The guards were so terrified they were like dead men," said Mary, one of the two women. "This angel told us that Jesus had risen from the dead. We saw the empty tomb and we ran to tell others."

The women claim that, as they were running to tell the other followers, Jesus himself met them.

"He said 'greetings' and to tell the others to go to Galilee where they would meet him."

Tomb Robbing

Their story has been dismissed by the authorities.

"There were no angels," they claimed. "What has happened here is a simple instance of tomb-robbing. Jesus's disciples came and took the body during the night."

When asked why several armed guards couldn't stop a few followers, most of whom were simple fishermen, the officer replied, "Well, you know what these people are like. They probably gave the guards a drugged haddock or something."

The Scroll asked to interview the guards who were on duty but we were told that they had "gone on holiday."

Jesus – A Statement

From the Office of the Governor

Dear Citizens,

You will no doubt have heard some of the rumours floating around Jerusalem at this time about this man Jesus.

I want to state on record and quite categorically that whatever might have happened – and we don't know whether anything has happened – but if it has, which it might have, then it was, in all probability nothing to do with me.

I wasn't even here at the time it happened, if it did happen. I'm not entirely sure where I was, but I was probably a long way away from here making very tough decisions which I'm very good at, actually.

**Everybody's friend,
Pontius Pilate**

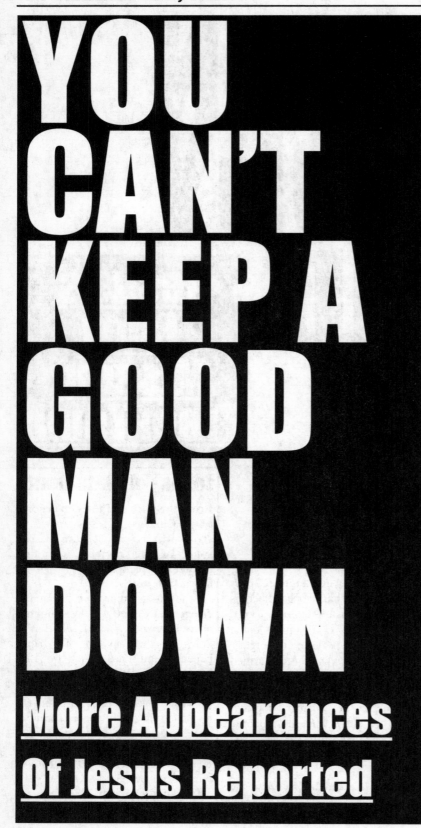

YOU CAN'T KEEP A GOOD MAN DOWN

More Appearances Of Jesus Reported

Further appearances of Jesus have been reported throughout the region.

On the Emmaus road two people were joined by a stranger who started to explain the scriptures to them. When they got to the inn where they were staying they sat down for a meal together and KNEW it was Jesus.

"It was the way he handled that loaf," said one of them.

"That and the fact that he disappeared into thin air immediately afterwards."

Breakfast

In a separate incident, he appeared to his disciples while they were fishing.

"We'd been fishing all night and caught nothing," said one. "Then this figure appeared on the seashore and told us to cast our nets the other side. Within minutes they were heaving with fish. We took the fish ashore and he cooked us breakfast."

Denial

The authorities were playing down the incidents.

"For a dead bloke, he doesn't half get about doesn't he?" said their spokesman. "I think you'll find this is a simple case of wish fulfilment. The bloke on the seashore was probably just one of those celebrity chefs. They're always cooking in weird places aren't they?

"And there are many cases of people mysteriously disappearing in restaurants. Usually when they get the bill."

Man Found Hanged

The body of the man found dead in a field outside Jerusalem has been identified as Judas, the disciple who handed Jesus over to the authorities. Police do not suspect foul play.

SCROLL LETTERS

SAY WHAT *YOU* WANT TO SAY

Is he or isn't he? Despite hundreds of sightings, reports of tombs breaking open and dead people walking the streets, and the news that his body has disappeared from the tomb, the authorities are refusing to acknowledge that something very unusual is happening. But are the people fooled? Here's a selection of your letters.

Dear *Scroll*,

As an undertaker, may I say how annoyed I am at all these dead people apparently walking around. I think it is very bad manners. When we have taken the trouble to lay someone out, they might at least stay dead.

I have been in the trade for thirty years and this is the first time I have ever heard of someone coming back from the dead – apart from Mrs Rabinowicz and that can be put down to some over-zealous relatives and the fact that the nurse who took her pulse had a broken watch.

Yours, gravely,
Nicodemus The Embalmer
"You Can Be Dead Sure of Nicodemus"

Dear Editor,

Just a short note to inform you officially that people don't come back from the dead and that any indication to the contrary in the pages of your paper will be taken as blasphemy.

Naturally I wouldn't dream of trying to manipulate the freedom of the press. Just bear in mind that the punishment for blasphemers is to be stoned to death, cut into pieces, burnt and then asked to leave the country.

With every good wish
Caiaphas
High Priest of Jerusalem

Dear Editor,

A few days ago I was a doubter like a lot of people. So when the rest of my colleagues said they had seen Jesus, I insisted on proof.

However, yesterday when we were together, he walked into the room. (Even though the door was locked.) One look was all it took to convince me that it was really him.

I hope this answers your questions,
Thomas Didymus

Dear *Scroll*,

I know the truth. There is a global conspiracy going on.

What I am saying is that nothing is what it seems. We don't know if Jesus ever died. I mean, I know he was crucified and stabbed in the side and all that and all the friends, relatives and enemies agree he died and that the soldiers made sure by killing him. *But what if they're all lying?*

I have to go now and get my acne seen to.

Burn this letter after you have read it.
Nathaniel

Dear Mr Scroll,

I think it could have happened! Only last year, Samuel my pet tortoise died. But this year, as soon as the warm weather arrived, he was back on his feet. So it can happen.

Yours sincerely,
Benjamin
P.S. My father says Samuel was only sleeping. But no one sleeps for four months! Apart from my brother, but he is an art student.

Sir,

You may be interested to know that I was the Centurion presiding over the crucifixion of Jesus. I have come to the conclusion that he was the Son of God. This was not an easy conclusion to come to, particularly as my wife is a keen worshipper of Jove. She has now gone home to her mother in disgust.

Yours, in wonder and gratitude at immediately answered prayer,
Romulus

Deer Eddytor,

One of my mates was on gard duty that nite and he hasent stoppt shaking yet. Somefink happened but he cant say wot, on account of how he has now been posted to Outer Hibernia.

They are covering it all up. (Not Outer Hibernia, I mean, wot happened.)

Yors sinseerly,
An Anonnymus Gard

FOLLOWERS OF JESUS FILLED WITH WIND

 ## Disciples Speak Different Languages

The crowds of visitors to Jerusalem witnessed an astonishing sight yesterday, as simple fishermen spoke to them in their native tongue.

These disciples of Jesus claim to have been visited by a spirit enabling them to speak different languages.

"We were all sitting together in this room, when suddenly there was this tremendous roaring sound of wind. This isn't that unusual, especially after the pilchards, but this was different."

Flame

After the wind it seemed that tongues of flame settled on their heads.

"It was weird," said another. "We were sitting there looking like giant birthday candles. Then we found we could speak different languages, so we rushed out and started talking to people.

Tourists

The city was full of tourists visiting at the festival of Pentecost, including Parthians, Medes, Egyptians and Libyans. Many reported having conversations in their own languages.

Continued on page 137

Continued from page 136

"It was incredible," said an Arab. "His accent was Galilean but I could understand him perfectly. He told me about his beliefs, then we discussed football for a while."

Drunk

Others, however, had different explanations. "Maybe they'd all taken very fast linguaphone courses," suggested one onlooker, while another believed a different kind of spirit was responsible.

"They were obviously drunk," he said. "I think we've all believed we can speak different languages after the spirit has visited us. Usually a spirit like vodka."

Leaders Warned

Two of the prime movers behind recent events in Jerusalem were arrested and warned yesterday.

Following the miraculous curing of a lame man, Peter (35) and John (30) were hauled before the religious authorities and charged with blasphemy, sedition, anti-Jewish rhetoric, lying, curing people without a permit and having badly styled beards.

They were let off with a warning which they completely ignored.

Thousands Sign Up

Their leader may be gone, but the followers of Jesus are still being heard. After a speech by their leader Peter, over 3,000 people joined their ranks in one day. Now the total number of followers has risen to over 5,000.

"It's trendy at the moment, but I wonder how many people will renew their subscriptions," said Gamaliel, one of the chief Pharisees. "A while ago it was Theudas, then Judas the Galilean. All of these attracted followers. But they didn't last. You mark my words, it will all be over in a few years' time."

Glory to God in the High Street
Appeal to Jesus's Followers to Spend More

Shopkeepers in Jerusalem are appealing to the new followers of Jesus to stop sharing everything.

"It's ridiculous," said a spokesman for the Jerusalem Board of Trade. "They live together, they have everything in common, and they've been selling all they have and giving the money away. I mean, it's just not natural."

Community

The followers are living in community and practising what they call the "breaking of bread".

"Admittedly they are buying a lot of bread and wine," said the spokesman. "But it would be nice to see them diversify a little. They could have the breaking of pasta, for instance. Just for a change."

Priests Appoint "Cult Tsar"
Saul To Hunt Heretics

Saul of Tarsus is the new "Cult Tsar" charged with spearheading the war against cults, blasphemies and generally stupid beliefs.

It is understood that this young Pharisee will start with the followers of Jesus before moving on to lesser known heresies such as black magic, Baal worship and macramé.

"I'm looking forward to the challenge," he said. "My only concern is to safeguard the purity of Judaism.

"If I have to kill people to do it, then so be it."

BEGINNING OF THE BIG BACKLASH

Stephen Stoned

Christians Persecuted

A vicious backlash against the followers of Jesus has been set in motion, following the execution of one of their members.

Stephen was stoned yesterday for blasphemy, after a court hearing in front of the High Priest.

"This cult is spreading like a rash," said Saul of Tarsus (23), who is heading up the government task force.

"It needs to be stamped out. Stoning is too good for them. But it will do until something more painful comes along."

Persecution

The stoning was followed by a general persecution, with houses smashed and burned, and followers of Jesus beaten up. Many of them have fled to outlying districts, or different countries.

"I don't care where they go," said Saul. "They can run but they can't hide."

"If you can't stand the heat, get out of the kitchen."

Spot The Apostle!

The persecution that Saul has inflicted on the followers of Jesus has led to many of the cult's leaders leaving Jerusalem.

Now you can enjoy their exodus with our new game, *Spot the Apostle.*

All you have to do is let us know when you see an apostle and you can win a cash prize!

Mrs M. of Samaria is our first winner, having spotted Philip.

"He wasn't hard to find," she says, "because he was standing in the city square performing miracles."

Play *Spot the Apostle* and you can be a winner with *The Scroll*!

CHAOS ON DAMASCUS ROAD

EXCLUSIVE

Did Aliens Cause Multi-chariot Pile-up?

Road networks around Israel were thrown into chaos yesterday as chariots were caught up in a pile-up on one of the country's busiest highways.

The Damascus Road was closed for several hours as the emergency services tried to clear the wreckage.

"People were simply driving too fast," said one traffic policeman. "When they had to stop quickly they just couldn't. There were bits of horse and camel everywhere."

According to police information, the chaos was caused by a white horse stopping suddenly in the fast lane. This caused the camel behind it to jack-knife and shed its load, blocking the carriageway.

Space Aliens

A police spokesman revealed the driver of the white horse had apparently had "a kind of vision".

"He claims to have been blinded by lights," reported one police spokesman. "However, we have ascertained that there were no vehicles coming in the opposite direction at the time: certainly none with their headlamps on."

Eye-witnesses, however, reported seeing a bright light and hearing some kind of voice.

"It was obviously a close encounter," said a spokesman for the UFO institute in Jerusalem. "There is quite clearly some kind of government cover-up going on. They don't want us to know the truth."

Police spokesmen refused to confirm or deny that a senior member of the anti-cult task force had been breathalysed and released on bail.

EUNUCH CALLS FOR CUTS

"Help The Poor" Says Convert

An Ethiopian Treasury Chief has called for cuts in government spending and more handouts to the poor.

The official, who is head of the Ethiopian Treasury, was speaking in the wake of a recent pilgrimage to Jerusalem where, "he started to see things in a different way".

"I was baptized in the River Jordan," he told a news conference. "I have become a follower of Jesus. I'd like to see us give more money away to those who need it."

The cult of Jesus is spreading rapidly throughout Israel, but this is thought to be the first indication of its presence in Ethiopia. Meanwhile, his government colleagues were playing down the Chancellor's statement.

"I can assure you this does not represent government fiscal policy," said the Prime Minister. "I can only assume he swallowed too much river water. There is a lot of nasty stuff floating in the Jordan these days. I hate to think what effect it's had on him."

Road Names "Too Confusing"

A postman has branded the Damascus road naming policy a disgrace after complaining it took him thirteen tries to find the right street.

"Road names aren't descriptive enough," he complained. "I had to deliver a letter to 13 Straight Street the other day. This is the Roman Empire, for heaven's sake. Every street is straight." He has called for roads to be given more descriptive names.

Among the names suggested are "Augustus Avenue", "Caesar Crescent" and Pontius Pilate Street". "Although admittedly the latter would only be appropriate for a cul-de-sac," he added.

PETER CLEANS UP HIS ACT

In a dramatic statement, overturning thousands of years of Jewish tradition, Peter has declared that there is no such thing as clean or unclean in the sight of God.

"God told me in a vision that there is no clean or unclean, just people who need something to believe in," he said.

His statement challenges the laws forbidding Jews to mix with other races, not to mention the strict Jewish dietary laws which forbid the eating of food such as pork, hare, ostrich and "Big Abdul's Triple-Strength Chipolata in Batter" from the stall outside the camel station.

Peter now expects to take the message to Gentile as well as Jew.

"No one is now beyond God's love," he said. "Not even Big Abdul."

They're Called Christians!

Report from Antioch reveals new name for followers of Jesus.

They've been called "followers of Jesus", "followers of the way", and "blood-sucking heretics who should be disembowelled" (although Saul has since retracted the last one).

But in Antioch they are being called "Christians".

"It's a good strong brand name," said one advertising executive. "But that in itself isn't enough."

"What they really need is a logo. I mean, they use this cross thing but that's terribly depressing. What about a nice flower? Or even a camel going through the eye of a needle."

Mascot

"You've got to pull the punters in. That's why I've developed a mascot – Damaris the Donkey Disciple. He's a little Christian donkey. I see a lot of marketing possibilities."

A leading "Christian" was sceptical.

"I see a long spell in a special ward," he said. "What really matters is the lifestyle, not the packaging."

THEY'VE LET ME OUT, NOW LET ME IN!

Peter Escapes Prison, But Can't Open The Front Door

Peter escaped from prison yesterday, but still couldn't get into his own prayer meeting.

As he tells it, he was released from prison by an angel and went straight to the home where a group of Christians were praying for his release. The trouble was, they wouldn't let him in!

"I got a bit excited when I saw him at the door," said the servant girl, Rhoda. "So I rushed back in to tell the others, without opening the front door first. I knew there was something I forgot."

Miracle

Most of the people inside refused to believe her. It was only when they came to the door and heard Peter hammering outside that they realized what had happened.

"Getting out of the prison wasn't the miracle," said Peter later. "It was getting the Christians to shut up and answer the front door."

STOP PRESS
Saul Converts

It has been revealed that the ex-Cult Tsar Saul has converted to Christianity.

He is keeping a very low profile for the moment. "He is so embarassed," said a friend, "that he'll soon be telling the world."

YOU SLIMY WORM

Death For The King Who Thought He Was God

Herod is dead. He was taken ill during a speech to a deputation from Tyre and Sidon.

During the speech the people acclaimed him with shouts of "It is a god speaking!" And even while they were shouting he was struck down.

Although he was rushed home he was already being eaten from the inside by WORMS!

"We don't know what really killed him," said a government official. "There were so many worms in his body, we didn't know whether to have the post mortem done by a surgeon or a gardener. It is clear they'd been chewing away at him for ages."

Justice

Others, however, saw it as divine justice.

"When a mere man claims to be a god he is asking for trouble," said an onlooker. "I mean look at these Roman Emperors. All of them claimed to be gods and all met horrible ends. They all end up as food for the worms. It's just with Herod the worms started snacking a bit earlier than usual."

Get Out Of That!
Paul Strikes Magician Blind

Paul, the Christian missionary who used to be known as Saul, has struck a Cypriot magician blind.

The Magician, Elymas, had tried to stop Paul speaking to the proconsul.

But Paul instantly struck him blind.

"Elymas was trying to get rid of the men, even though the Proconsul wanted to hear what they had to say," said a witness. "I think Elymas had some card tricks he wanted to do.

Fraud

"Anyway, Paul called him a fraud, imposter, son of the devil and enemy of goodness. And that was some of the nicer things he said.

"After that Elymas was struck blind. Now he can't read the tea leaves, or do that terribly clever thing when he saws the vestal virgin in half. I think it's only temporary, but we can always hope."

WHO'S A PRETTY BOY THEN?

Greeks Unimpressed By "Paul The Parrot"

Paul, the famous Christian convert, has been called a "parrot" by some of the leading Greek philosophers.

The missionary is on a trip to Athens, where his teaching has met stern opposition, but also some success.

Weird

"Some of the people listening to him called him a 'parrot'," said one listener. "In Greece we call people that who talk a lot. Others thought he was a propagandist for some weird gods."

In Athens, Paul (44) has found a very different audience to that which he is used to. "These people like to talk about ideas," he said.

"In fact they don't do much else. Admittedly some of them haven't agreed with what I've said, but at least they only laugh at you. Back home, they express criticism by chucking great lumps of stone at you."

Statue

Paul used a famous statue – the Statue of the Unknown God – to illustrate his talk. However, his statement that Jesus rose from the dead caused some members of the crowd to jeer him.

"These people are broadly split into two camps," said Paul. "The Stoics believe that life is to be endured, the Epicureans believe that life is to be enjoyed. The Stoics are fed up and the Epicureans are over fed. All I wanted to do was show them that there is another way."

Synagogue Ruler Attacked As Case Is Thrown Out

A synagogue leader who had Paul arrested was beaten up by his own supporters following the collapse of his case.

Sosthenes (54) had Paul hauled before Gallo, the proconsul in Corinth. But the case was dismissed.

The Jews were so angry at the failure of their case they turned on Sosthenes and beat him. He was taken to hospital.

"He's not doing very well," said his wife. "He's badly bruised and of course, his case has been quashed."

Paul came to Corinth after Athens. He is working as a tent-maker by day and preaching at night.

"I intend to go on preaching," he said. "And can I interest you in our two-berth backpacker's special with built in ground-sheet?"

DON'T TOUCH OUR DI!

Silversmiths Lead Riot in Ephesus

Silversmiths in Ephesus have been rioting to protect their interests, in the wake of the increasing spread of Christianity.

"If this pernicious faith continues growing they will take away everything that makes this place special," thundered Demetrius the chief silversmith.

"People come from all around the world to see the Temple of Diana and worship at her shrine. She's the people's goddess. We must preserve her."

The silversmiths make most of their money by providing images of Diana for the booming tourist trade.

Among products available in Ephesus's market place are Diana mugs, Diana medals and "I ♥ Diana" stickers for the back of their chariots.

Riot

The protest came to a head recently, when the silversmiths staged a riot in protest at the Christian idea that man-made gods are not gods at all.

"This threatens our fundamental democratic rights," said Demetrius (47). "I know that the goddess has never answered any of our prayers, or, indeed done anything at all, but she's ours. It's a basic human right to get man-made goddesses out of all proportion."

Obsession

Others claim that Ephesus is obsessed with Diana.

"This place has gone Diana mad," said one visitor. "You can't pick up a paper without her image falling out. There are thousands of scrolls about her and even a tacky drama documentary about her life. I think it might be time we got things into perspective."

The visitor was about to say more when he was felled by a silversmith's hammer.

PAUL IS ARRESTED
"I Thought He Was A Revolting Egyptian" Admits Tribune

Paul has been arrested on the steps of the temple at Jerusalem. He was attacked by an angry mob and eventually taken into custody for his own protection.

So great was the noise, that when the tribune came to sort out the riot, he had no idea who Paul actually was.

"I thought he was the bloke who led that revolt in the desert," he admitted. "You know, Abdul the Mad Sausage Man. It was only later on he said that he was a Roman citizen. It was just as well, I was about to have him flogged – just to help with routine enquiries, you understand."

Saved

The next day, Paul was taken down to the Jewish council where he promptly caused another riot by preaching what he believed. Once again, the Tribune had to step in and save him.

"Every time he opens his gob people want to smack it," said the Centurion.

"I mean, he was even punched by the High Priest. If irritating people was an Olympic sport this guy would be world class. He could irritate for Israel and win the gold medal every time."

Paul Intends To Appeal To Caesar

Amidst all the turmoil over his arrest and subsequent trial, it is rumoured that Paul has appealed to Caesar to have his case heard.

This right, only available to Roman citizens, means that he will eventually be transferred to Rome.

"The sooner he gets out of here the better," said the new governor Porcius Festus. "Both King Agrippa and I have heard him speak and we have decided to ship him to Rome. If you ask me, he's an accident just waiting to happen."

ROME SWEET ROME

Paul Arrives In The Eternal City

Paul, the famous Christian missionary and all-round trouble-maker, arrived in Rome yesterday after a journey of many months.

Along the way he was shipwrecked and bitten by a poisonous snake, in quick succession. The snake has since died.

He will now live under house arrest in Rome until his trial can be heard.

"I will be very busy," said Paul. "I have a case to prepare and a lot of letters to write. I've got to write to the Colossians, the Ephesians, and the Philippians. And I also want to send a postcard to Philemon."

Paul has become famous for his letters to churches throughout Asia Minor. Many churches are now basing their understanding of the Christian faith on Paul's "epistles", as they are known.

"I'm just trying to make sense of everything that's happened," said Paul. "Obviously not all my letters are equally important. There are several to Aunty Beryl that are merely thanking her for my birthday present."

Future

"I think he will probably be released this time around," said a source. "There are no real charges and Nero is more interested in his violin practice than religious law. I know Paul has plans to travel as far as Spain. After that, who knows? Everything should be OK providing Nero doesn't go as nutty as the other Emperors.

"But there's not much chance of that!"

It's All Ship-Shape

The captain of a ship about to leave for Crete and Malta has defended his ship against accusations it is in bad repair.

"This baby is in perfect shape," said Captain Aristarchus (55). "She's as solid as a rock," he added, not very appropriately.

Faults

Authorities are not so sure.

"There are loads of faults," said one inspector. "Slack rigging, creaking joints and a faulty bottom – and that's just the captain. The ship is even worse."

The ship will carry mainly trade goods, but some political and religious prisoners for trial in Rome.

Cake

"This journey will be a piece of cake," answered the captain. "What could possibly go wrong?"

"Well, all sorts of things could happen," said the inspector. "The ship could be caught in a hurricane off Crete and spend the next fourteen days in a desperate attempt to outrun the storm, during which time all the goods and equipment have to be thrown overboard, before the passengers have to swim to shore lashed to bits of wood, as the ship runs aground at Malta, and everyone is miraculously preserved," he conjectured.

"But that's just a guess."

SCROLL MONEY

Taking Care of Your Shekels

That's A Bit Rich!

Christians Warned Against Bias to the Wealthy

Christian meetings are warned against pandering to rich people and ignoring the poor, in a report from James, the brother of Jesus.

Writing to Christians throughout the world, James warns them of the dangers of preferring those with money.

"God has chosen the poor to be rich in faith," said James. "It's not right that some assemblies of Christians are reserving the best seats for the rich."

Market Place

The Christian meetings – or "churches" as they are called – have struck back at his criticism.

"Look, we're all in a market place here," said Rev. Hiram Cheap, Pastor of the First Church on the Make, Antioch. "I think what we have to do is offer quality and added value to our customers. If that means splitting the seating into club class and economy seats, then that's what we'll do."

Hiram's "church" offers a duty-free trolley, a three-course menu and a choice of aperitifs before the service. It recently made headlines as the first church to be listed on the stock exchange.

"We're not against the poor," explained Hiram. "It's just they've never got any money. Personally I think the rich are more in need of saving. That's why we offer them the better seats, so they can hear the sermon better."

James, however, refused to acknowledge this argument.

"Those who are rich will weep and wail," he said. "Their wealth will rot and the moths will eat their clothes. 'Blessed are the poor,' if I may quote a member of my family."

Power

His arguments come as senior economists predict a rosy future for the church.

"If it carries on growing the way it is, it will be a huge multi-national corporation before long," said one. "It's all very well being pure of heart when you are poor and weak. The real question is what the church is going to do when it is rich and powerful. I'll bet James' letter won't be half so popular then."

Your Holiday Shekel

Here's what the Jewish Shekel will buy abroad:

ROME: 30 Denarii

BABYLON: 4 Pot Plants

PHOENICIA: 1.75 Talents

GREECE: 23.7 Drachmas

BRITANNIA: A bit of woad and a lump of coal

HISPANIA: 3 litres of olive oil, a large jug of sangria

GAUL: 40 heads of garlic

ASSYRIA: A small forest, several buildings and quite possibly the inn-keeper's daughter in marriage

BELGIUM: 3 ECUs (Etruscan Currency Units)

Shares: The Top Performers

Retail & Entertainment		
John Mark & Spencer	630.0	+19.0
Romo Disney	79.0	-1.2
Masada United F.C.	156.0	+4.1
Laura Ashkelon	39.5	-2.0
Sandals	898.0	+28.0
Herods Department Store	154.5	-0.5
Food & Drink		
Big Abdul's Sausage Inc.	1510.0	+2.0
Hibernian & Nile Brewers	714.5	+19.5
Grand Mesopotamian	548.0	+9.0
Festus Frozen Food	112.5	-11.0
Travel		
CamelTrack	1015.0	+20.0
Britannia Boatways	559.0	+22.0
Rhodes Royce	240.0	+3.0
Galleyslaves 'R' Us	484.0	-0.5
Essene Petroleum	124.0	-5.0
GalileeTunnel	5.5	-40.5
Banks & Building Societies		
Alliance & Lebanon	740.0	+10.0
Nazareth Westminster	885.0	-13.0
Ba'albek & Bethlehem	3110.0	+8.5
Miscellaneous		
First Church on the Make	2.5	-312.0
Microbeast	100.4	+0.4
Cable and Whiplash	532.5	-5.5
Cosy-Fit Tents	321.8	-2.3
Anoint & Go	120.8	-7.2

APOCALYPSE NOW

Horsemen Ride Through...

Plagues Hit The Earth...

Armageddon Announced...

Turkey Win Eurovision Song Contest

Is This The End?

You Can Lead A Horse To Slaughter
Four Horsemen Ride The Skies

Where their hooves fell, the sun turned black.

Their horses were monstrous, wild-eyed stallions, bringing with them death, disease, despair and many other things beginning with 'd'.

Yes, the four horsemen of the apocalypse – war, famine, plague and badly fitting shoes – have been unleashed onto the earth.

"I don't like the look of them at all," said a vet. "Those horses have something wrong with them if you ask me.

"For a start, there's the colours. I mean, who ever heard of a red horse? And that pale one looks like death."

"The pale horse *is* death," said a theology expert. "That's the point."

End Times

"We are in the end times," said one viewer. "Make no doubt about it, things are going to get a lot worse before they get better."

Given that we have already had earthquakes, fire, stars falling from the sky and a plague that wiped out a third of the earth's population, this does not appear to be comforting news.

"This is the end of the world," confirmed another expert. "It's all downhill from here."

The Beast Is Yet To Come
Seven-headed Beast Emerges

A huge, seven-headed beast has come out of the sea. Reports are confused as to the appearance of this phenomenon. Some people say it looks like a leopard, others a bear, or a lion.

One particularly confused old geezer thought it looked like a Teletubby.

The beast has been breathing out blasphemies against God and has attracted large numbers of followers already.

"He's kind of cute," said one fan. "In a huge, horrific, ten-horned sort of way."

More

Others are already talking of the follow up, or Beast 2 as it is known.

"Any month now we should see another beast," said an expert. "He will look like a lamb, but speak like a dragon. A bit like Louis Armstrong in a sheepskin coat. He will deceive us all."

Mark

One of the features of the second beast is that he will control all commerce.

"Everyone who wants to trade will have to have the mark of the beast on their heads," said a spokesman for MicroBeast Inc. "We don't like to think of it as a monopoly, it's more a secure trading environment."

The number on the heads will be 666.

"Unless you're standing upside down," said the spokesman. "In which case you'll call the fire brigade."

Foretold

For many people all this will come as no surprise.

"It was all in Revelation," said one expert. "Although I have to admit we didn't think it would literally be like this. I guess we thought it was all going to be more a sign language sort of thing."

★ ★ ★ ★ ★

Armageddon Out Of Here!
Gigantic Explosion Splits Earth

The world has been rocked by an enormous explosion.

"Whole islands have just sunk into nothingness," said a geography expert. "Mountains have been razed to the ground."

In some parts of the world huge hail stones over 40 kg in weight have been falling from the sky.

"I'm not sure how long these will be falling for," said a weatherman. "My best advice is to run away. Or buy a very strong umbrella."

The disaster came as the Kings of the world gathered on the plains of Armageddon.

"This just about caps it," said one. "We've had the beasts, the horses, and now great lumps are falling on us. I wish the whole thing was ended."

★ ★ ★ ★ ★

NEW HEAVEN
★ AND A ★
NEW EARTH
God Takes Back Control And Creates Again

In a move that brings back memories of the very start, God has created a new heaven and a new earth.

"God is going to live with men for ever more," said a voice from heaven. "This is the way it will end."

The move proves a fitting conclusion to the story of God's relationship with mankind.

"This is how it should have been all along," said an angel. "Just think, if it hadn't gone wrong in the Garden, it would have been like this all the time. No deaths, no disease, none of that mayhem and carnage that has filled all those back issues of *The Scroll*."

The new heaven and earth contains the new Jerusalem. And running through the main street the river of life.

"The tree is back as well," said the angel, pointing to the Tree of Life.

Beginning And End

"I am the Alpha and the Omega," said God (∞) at a press conference, referring to the first and last letters of the Greek alphabet. "The beginning and the end," he added helpfully.

"There will be no more tears, no more death, no more mourning, or sadness, or pain. The old world is gone."

And so the world ends as it began: God and man in harmony.

As God himself put it, "I've started so I'll finish."

The Scroll

Please address all correspondence to our new offices:
**12 Clear-Gold Street
The Seventh Set of
Pearly Gates
New Jerusalem**

SCROLL BACK ISSUES
Looking for an old story? Here's where you find it.

Hello World – Genesis 1

Adam Names The Animals – Genesis 2: 19–20

Meat-free Diet – Genesis 1:29–30

Thank God for Sunday – Genesis 2:2–3

He And She – Genesis 2:21–24

Trees Of Good And Evil – Genesis 2:16–17

Serpent Questions Fruit Policy – Genesis 3:1–5

Would You Adam And Eve It! – Genesis 3

Clothing Invented – Genesis 3:7, 21

Punishment Outlined – Genesis 3: 14–24

Oi! Mind That Flaming Sword! – Genesis 3:24

Cain In The Neck – Genesis 4:1–8

Judgement On Cain – Genesis 4:9–16

Arking Mad! – Genesis 6 & 7

Land Ahoy! – Genesis 8

Rainbow – Genesis 9:1–17

Grape Expectations – Genesis 9:20–21

Towering Confusion! – Genesis 11:1–9

Here Today, Gone Gomorrah! – Genesis 19:1–29

Not Even Ten Good Men! – Genesis 18:16–33

Lot's Wife Is A-salt-ed – Genesis 19:25–26

Why Not Take My Daughters? –
   Genesis 19:6–8

90-Year-Old Gives Birth – Genesis 17:15–22 &
   21:1–7

Ishmael Leaves Home – Genesis 21:8–21

Back From The Brink! – Genesis 22:1–18

Israel Gets The Hump – Genesis 24

Abraham Dies – Genesis 25:7–11

Birthright Robbery – Genesis 25:29–34

Blessing In Disguise – Genesis 27

Two Wife Sentences! – Genesis 29

Would Ewe Believe It? – Genesis 30:25–43

Jacob Transfers – Genesis 31

Jacob Injured In Bizarre Wrestling Match –
   Genesis 32:23–33

Re-united! – Genesis 33:1–11

Was This The Unkindest Cut Of All? –
   Genesis 34

Scroll Spot – Name Change – Genesis 35:9–10

Could They Be Lion? – Genesis 37

Advertisement – Genesis 37:28, 36

Are You-dah Father? – Genesis 38

You Sex Slave! – Genesis 39:1–20

Dear Osiris... – Genesis 40

Canaan Refugees Accused Of Spying –
   Genesis 42

Oh Brother! – Genesis 45

Pharaoh In "Nilegate" Land Acquisition Scandal
   – Genesis 47

Jacob Dies – Genesis 49 & 50

Kill Them All! – Exodus 1

Princess And The Basket Case – Exodus 2

Will You Listen To That Flamin' Bush! –
   Exodus 3

Twice The Workload – Exodus 5

Snakes Alive! – Exodus 7

River Of Blood – Exodus 7

Hop It Moses! – Exodus 8

Final Demand – Exodus 9 & 10

The Dead Of The Night – Exodus 11

Special Feast – Exodus 12

Gotcha! – Exodus 14

After 430 Years, The Israelites Leave – Exodus
   12:31–41

To The Manna Born – Exodus 16

Moses Finds Water – Exodus 17

New Management Structure – Exodus 18

Is That My Donkey You're Coveting? – Exodus 20

All Bow To The Cow! – Exodus 32

How Now Gold Cow? – Exodus 32

Keep On Taking The Tablets – Exodus 33

God In A Box – Exodus 37

You're Looking Radiant Tonight, Moses –
    Exodus 34:29–35

It'll Be All White On The Night – Numbers 12

No Honey Please, We're Chickens – Numbers 13

Forty Years On – Numbers 14

Wisdom From The Wise – Nazirite

Amorite Bees Sting Israelites – Numbers
    14:39–45

Moses Retires – Deuteronomy 31

Spies Found In Prostitute's House – Joshua 2

Atishoo! Atishoo! Wall Fall Down! – Joshua 6

"Ai" Feel Really Stupid – Joshua 8

Joshua Dies – Joshua 24

Over The Hilt And Far Away! – Judges 3:12–30

Sisera Pegs Out – Judges 4

Deborah – An Inspiration To Us All – Judges
    4:1–11

Gide-on My Son! – Judges 7

Gideon Beats Midian – Judges 4:8–25

Night Of The Fox – Judges 14

From Jawbone To War-bone! – Judges 15

Hair Today – Gone Tomorrow! – Judges 16

Sightless Samson Brings The House Down –
    Judges 16:23–31

We Want A King! – 1 Samuel 8

That's Saul Folks! – 1 Samuel 9

Samuel Retires – 1 Samuel 12

Mishmash At Michmash – 1 Samuel 13 & 14

I'll Kill You All! – 1 Samuel 17

The Fall Of A Giant – 1 Samuel 17

Giant Slayer Tipped As King – 1 Samuel 16

It's Time For Me To Dis-A-Spear! –
    1 Samuel 19

Let Off On The Loo – 1 Samuel 24

David Has Killed His Tens Of Thousands –
    1 Samuel 18:6–9

Witch Way Now? – 1 Samuel 28

Saul Alone – 1 Samuel 31

David Is King – 2 Samuel 2

King David And The Wife Of Bath –
    2 Samuel 11

General Killed In Heroic Battle – 2 Samuel 11

First His Wife, Then His Life – 2 Samuel 12

Officials Fear For The King's Health – 2 Samuel
    12:15–23

A Death In The Family – 2 Samuel 13

It's War, My Son! – 2 Samuel 15

Stone Me! – 2 Samuel 16:5–14

Absalom Hangs Out – 2 Samuel 18

King Weeps For His Son – 2 Samuel 18:19–19:8

A Nation Mourns – 1 Kings 1

Last Days Blighted By Further Intrigue –
    1 Kings 2

Joab Kill-ted At The Altar – 1 Kings 2:26–35

Let's Split, Baby! – 1 Kings 3:16–28 & 1 Kings
    4:29–34

Solomon To Build Temple – 1 Kings 5

Solomon The Architect – 1 Kings 7

Here Sheba Comes! – 1 Kings 10

Doing The Splits – 1 Kings 12

No Baal Games Allowed – 1 Kings 18

It Could Be Jehu – 1 Kings 19

Elijah Appoints Successor – 1 Kings 19:19–21

That's Vine!– 1 Kings 21

Burn Rubber Baby – 2 Kings 2

Elisha Grins And Bears It – 2 Kings 2:23–25

How The Mighty Are Fallen – 2 Kings 9

Hard Drive – 2 Kings 9:20

What's On – Highlights – 2 Kings 23:1–3

Prophet Hooks Up With A Hooker – Hosea 2

Ezekiel Sees Dancing Bones – Ezekiel 37

Hi Ho, Hi Ho, To Babylon We Go! – 2 Kings 24

Phew, Not A Scorcher! – Daniel 3

Dream Reader Gets Top Post – Daniel 2

That'll Come In Handy – Daniel 5

Is The King A Looney? – Daniel 4:28–33

Daniel Still Dreaming – Daniel 7

When The Writing Was On The Wall – Daniel 5: 30–31

Our Lions Are Vegetarian – Daniel 6

Please Release Me, Let Me Go – Nehemiah 1

Local Councils Opposed to Building Scheme – Nehemiah 4

Cyrus Spells Freedom! – Ezra 1

Having A Whale Of A Time! Jonah

Teenager In Love – Matthew 1:18–25

Keeping It In The Family – Daniel 3

Utter Non-Census – Luke 1

A Stable Relationship – Luke 2

While Shepherds Watched – Luke 2:8–20

Wise Men Look For A Star – Matthew 2:1–12

Slaughter Of The Innocents! – Matthew 2:13–18

Snakes Alive! – Luke 3

Trouble And Strife – Luke 3:19–20

Locust Gratin Please – Matthew 3

John Baptizes Cousin – Matthew 3: 13–17

Pie In The Sky – Matthew 5

Jesus Come Home – Mark 3

That'll Come In Handy – Matthew 12

It's All Too Much! – Matthew 19:16–30

Jesus Pigs Out – Luke 8: 26–39

Ding Dong! Kingdom Calling! – Matthew 10

Tax Collectors Call For Code Of Conduct – Matthew 9:9–13 & Luke 19

How To Get Ahead In Dancing – Matthew 14: 1–12

Jesus Feeds Five Thousand – Matthew 14: 13–21

Trees A Jolly Good Fellow – Luke 1

Back From The Grave – John 11:1–44

Adulteress Loses Stones – John 8:1–11

Hero's Welcome – Matthew 21:1–11

A Pain In The Temple – Matthew 21:12–17

High Level Talks About Supposed Messiah – John 11:45–57

Jesus Has Smelly Feet – John 12

Jesus Arrested – Luke 22:47–53

Free The Jerusalem One! – Luke 23

"My Hands Are Clean" – Luke 23

Mystery In Courtyard – Luke 22:54–62

Shake Rattle And Roll – Luke 23:44–49

It Is Finished – Luke 23:26–49

You Seen Anybody Round Here? – Luke 24: 1–12

You Can't Keep A Good Man Down – Luke 24:13–49

Man Found Hanged – Matthew 27:1–10

Scroll Letters, Centurion – Luke 23:47–49, Thomas – John 20: 24–29

Followers Of Jesus Filled With Wind – Acts 2

Thousands Sign Up – Acts 2: 41–47

Glory To God in the High Street – Acts 2: 42–47

Leaders Warned – Acts 4

Beginning of the Backlash – Acts 7

Spot The Apostle – Acts 8:1–8

Chaos On Damascus Road – Acts 9

Eunuch Calls For Cuts – Acts 8:26–40

Road Names "Too Confusing" – Acts 9:11

Peter Cleans Up His Act – Acts 10

They're Called "Christians" – Acts 11: 25 & 26

They've Let Me Out, Now Let Me In! – Acts 12

You Slimy Worm – Acts 12:19–25

Get Out Of That! – Acts 13: 4–12

Who's A Pretty Boy Then? – Acts 17

Synagogue Ruler Attacked – Acts 18

Don't Touch Our Di! – Acts 19

Paul Is Arrested – Acts 21

Ne-phew! – Acts 23:12–22

Paul Will Appeal To Caesar – Acts 24

Everything's Ship-shape – Acts 27 & 28

Rome Sweet Rome – Acts 28:11–16

That's A Bit Rich! – James 2:1–7 & 5:1–6

You Can Lead A Horse To Slaughter – Revelation 6

The Beast Is Yet To Come – Revelation 13

Armageddon Out Of Here – Revelation 16

New Heaven And New Earth – Revelation 21